0069587

DATE DUE

NOV 2 8 1995	

QL
737
S63
D54
1992

Dietz, Tim.

The call of the
siren.

$15.95

T H E
Call of the Siren

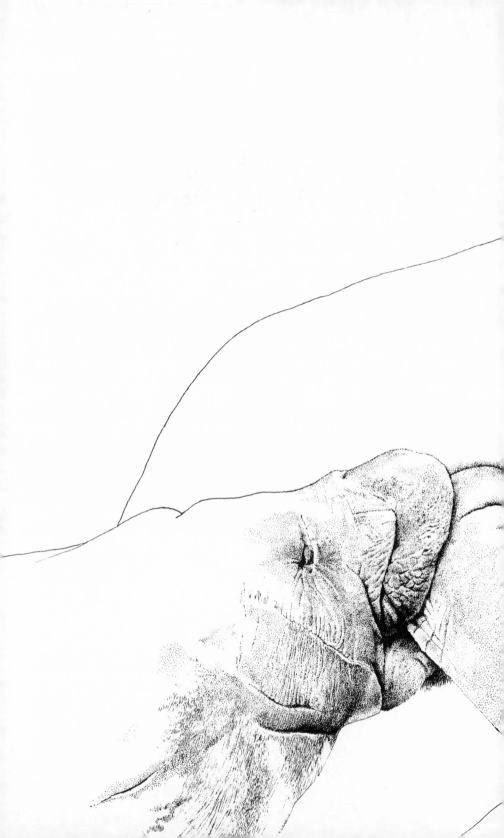

THE
Call of the Siren
MANATEES AND DUGONGS

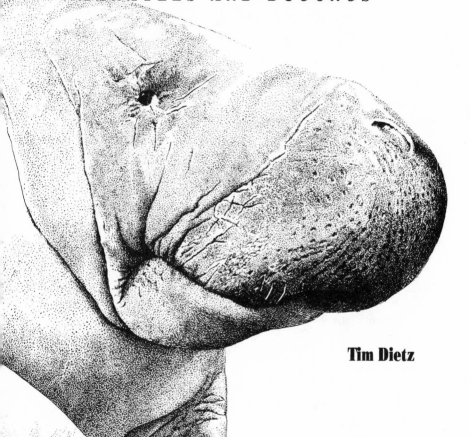

Tim Dietz

Illustrations by Walter Gaffney-Kessell

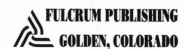

FULCRUM PUBLISHING
GOLDEN, COLORADO

Library of Congress Cataloging-in-Publication Data

Dietz, Tim.
  The call of the siren : manatees and dugongs / Tim Dietz.
    p. cm.
  Includes bibliographical references and index.
  ISBN 1-55591-104-8
  1. Manateees—Florida. 2. Dugong—Florida. 3. Endangered species—Florida. 4. Wildlife conservation—Florida. I. Title.
QL737.S63D54 1992
599.5'5'09759—dc20
                                                          92-53036
                                                          CIP

Printed in the United States of America

0   9   8   7   6   5   4   3   2

Fulcrum Publishing
350 Indiana Street, Suite 350
Golden, Colorado 80401-5093

To my parents-in-law,
Richard and Jeannette Collins,
for the love they share
and the joy they bring.

C O N T E N T S

ACKNOWLEDGMENTS

In the course of researching and writing this book, I've been very fortunate to meet and work with many fine individuals who took the time to allow an interview, provide information, offer suggestions, or assist in researching a specific topic. In particular, I offer thanks to Walter Gaffney-Kessell for his remarkably creative mind, endurance in the face of many obstacles, and the special design of this book; Judith Delaney Vallee, executive director of the Save the Manatee Club, for her thoughtfulness and bountiful supply of information; Bill Taylor and Christine Fleuriel of the Dana-Farber Cancer Institute in Boston for their help in unlocking the secrets to the Harvard University Libraries; Wayne Hartley for taking the time to introduce me to the winter residents of Blue Spring; J. Ross Wilcox at Florida Power & Light for his generosity in providing research material and time for interviews; Thomas O'Shea at the National Ecology Research Center in Gainesville for his prompt response to my inquiries; Tony and Nancy Viehmann for their spirit; Becca Moore, Dan Odell, and Vic Aderholt at Sea World for their time; and the Embassy of Australia in Washington, DC, the South Florida Museum, and the Conservation Foundation of the World Wildlife Fund.

It was truly a pleasure to work with Pat Frederick, whose delightful personality, editorial skills and careful guidance played a vital role in the development of this book.

I am also forever grateful for the opportunity to enjoy the friendship of Tony and Joyce Jonaitis who provided special companionship and hospitality on my many trips to Florida. To these two spirited adventurers I owe a special debt of gratitude.

Finally, to my wife Kathy and our daughters Lani and Erin: Thank you for your love, patience, encouragement, and heartwarming smiles every day of every year.

PREFACE

The raucous parade of motorboats had stilled for the time being. On the bow of a tattered aluminum boat, I was staring into the clear waters of Crystal River, watching the distinctively massive form of a manatee shimmer in shades of pale green as it passed beneath. The luminous sky was punctuated here and there by the silhouettes of birds in flight. I could hear a distant squawking of seagulls and the splash of a pelican plunging headlong into the water in search of food. A delicate breeze felt warm on my face as I watched the manatee drift away slowly. At that moment I wished that everyone could experience a similarly intense few seconds of nature in its purest form. But, too quickly, it passed, leaving only a memory.

When I decided to write a book about manatees, dugongs, and their extinct cousin, Steller's sea cow, I wanted to capture in writing as many of these moments as possible while introducing readers to the wonderful world of these little known creatures because they too have passed or are passing. Steller's sea cow is already extinct. And manatees and dugongs are perched on the brink of the abyss.

Chances are their disappearance off the face of the earth wouldn't turn many heads. Few people are even aware that they exist at all. But their loss would mean more than most of us can fully appreciate. Like many plants and creatures in similar situations, they are the measure of the earth's health. Florida and its manatee population, in particular, represent a microcosm of the dilemma facing this planet—too many people, too little space.

The Nature Conservancy notes that twelve of Florida's eighty-one distinctive ecosystems, ranging from the temperate pine forest of the northern Panhandle to the tropical coral reefs of the southern Florida Keys, are considered critically endangered. The state's natural areas disappearing beneath concrete and asphalt at the rate of 260 square miles a year. Federal and state agencies consider 117 animal and 182 plant species to be either endangered, threatened, or in need of special protection. And still people come at the rate of over one thousand new residents a day. In a state where recreation and tourism drives the economy, there's little support for a silent, harmless marine mammal whose ancestors date back to the Eocene epoch over 55 million years ago.

But Florida is only part of the story. Manatees and dugongs range widely over Earth's waters, and their history is intermingled with the complex and evolving tale of human history. They have been loved and honored, but more often they have been abused, even feared. Yet they endure; gentle, placid animals that existed in peace with their environment for millions of years before the coming of man.

The National Science Foundation recently estimated that at the present rate of extinction, over a quarter or more of Earth's species will disappear. It is a discouraging statistic, but not a hopeless fact. Even today, as long as small pockets of the natural world continue to exist, changes for the better can be initiated.

It is my hope that by introducing you to the fascinating world of manatees and dugongs I will spark an interest that will help prevent them from becoming a part of these discouraging statistics. We need manatees and dugongs and the rich biological diversity they represent. And we owe the pleasure of their company to future generations.

Tim Dietz
Kennebunk, Maine

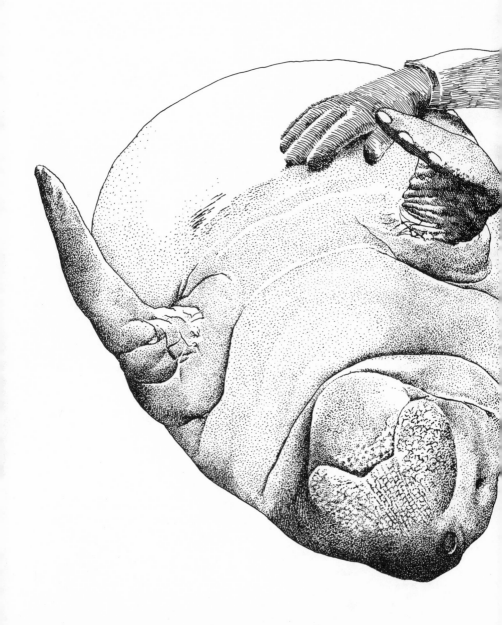

THE SIREN'S CALL

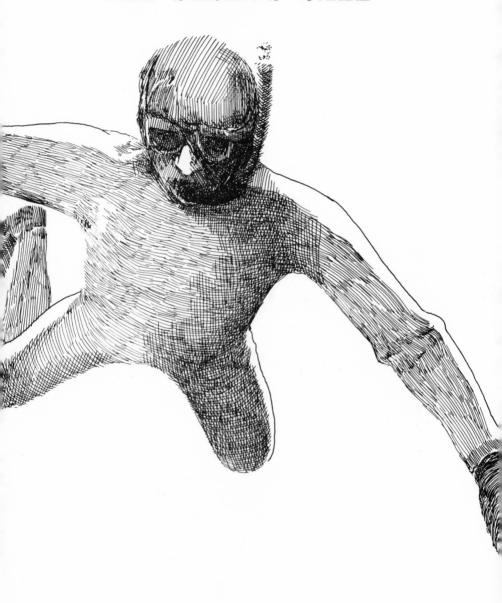

FIRST ENCOUNTERS

As I sped northward in my car on Route 19, dodging the reckless lane-jumpers and braking at the innumerable stoplights spanning each intersection, I found myself glancing at the meager remains of subtropical foliage left alongside the road.

The blur of passing scenery and the low, steady hum of the car's engine had a soothing, almost hypnotic effect on me. My thoughts drifted back to another era, centuries before. I imagined Spanish explorers hacking their way through a lush, subtropical setting bursting with the bold, emerald colors of an N. C. Wyeth painting; a steamy landscape laced with untamed foliage and mysterious, fetid swamps. Back then Florida must have seemed like a rough jewel, hiding its secrets beneath an inhospitable exterior, bursting with the promise of the unknown. Times, though, have changed.

I first came to Florida in the early 1970s, when the state was just shaking its image as a sleepy haven for retirees and beginning to boom as a business and financial center of the Sun Belt states. Walt Disney had discovered the spacious interior. The young and upwardly mobile were beginning to opt for sunny skies and warm temperatures year-round. As scores of people moved southward, the state entered an era of unprecedented growth that has continued to this day.

Now most of coastal Florida is one endless development after another: shopping centers, condominiums, fast food outlets, and more convenience stores and gas stations than people, or so it seems. Whatever palm trees and palmetto bushes remain on the coast are usually landscaped into tiny oases of vegetation designed to offset the severity of acres of asphalt parking lots.

This is hardly the setting in which you'd expect to find one of nature's true marvels. But I had come here to do just that. My destination was the Crystal River National Wildlife Refuge, the winter home of a creature of myth as much as of reality, an animal who seems more the stuff of fantasy than any Florida tourist attraction. Soon I would be exploring the crystalline springs that play seasonal host to the remarkable West Indian manatee.

Huge, slow-moving, and disarmingly docile, these marine mammals look like softer, more cuddlesome versions of walruses minus the tusks. Christopher Columbus was the first European to write about these animals in the New World, describing them, in the journal of his historic voyage across the Atlantic in 1492, as *serenas* (mermaids), although he prudently added that "they were not as beautiful as they are painted."

Despite the fact that adult manatees can grow to over 12 feet in length and weigh up to 3,500 pounds, they are completely harmless and easy to approach. The Crystal River refuge is one of the best—perhaps *the* best—spots to meet manatees face to face. The refuge encompasses nine islands surrounded by the sparkling spring-fed waters of Kings Bay, a popular winter gathering ground for manatees, who require a constant 74-degree water temperature to survive in colder weather.

In mid-winter, when the air and the offshore water temperatures drop, manatees congregate by the hundreds in the bay, luring divers and snorkelers from all over the country, much like the sirens of ancient mythology lured seafarers. But, unlike their mythological counterparts, manatees want nothing more than a belly scratch, a back rub, or a little playful wrestling from terrestrial visitors. By all accounts it seems to be a blissful relationship. Manatees thrive in the warm, food-rich waters of the bay while divers enjoy the opportunity to frolic with some of Florida's oldest and most gentle residents. But there's trouble in paradise.

Despite protection from state and federal legislation, the estimated population of 1,856 manatees in Florida is under environmental siege. Growing coastal development and the resulting increase in boat traffic is making the very waters that historically protected the animal, deadly. A record 206 manatees died in the state during 1990, 174 during 1991, the victims of slashing boat propellers, crushing flood-control gates, poachers who still kill the animals for food, and man-made waste products such as floating plastics ingested by the mammals. It's a classic confrontation between man and wildlife, and a search for its resolution is causing a growing furor extending beyond the limits of the manatee's southeastern home.

I had come to Florida to meet the peaceful source of this controversy. My lifelong interest in marine mammals had been focused primarily on whales, but the growing plight of the manatee, and its striking similarity to the whale preservation issue, intrigued me. Like whales, manatees are remarkably gentle marine mammals that hover on the brink of extinction as a result of overzealous hunting and drastic environmental changes. Even with stringent protection, all marine mammals now face an uncertain future complicated by perplexing environmental questions.

In an earlier conversation with Pat Hagen, then the manager of the Chassahowitzka National Wildlife Refuge which encompasses the Crystal River refuge, I was told that the early morning hours offered the best chance to encounter manatees in the southern half of Kings Bay, just off Banana Island. According to Pat, the water would have less silt, which is usually stirred up by scores of snorkelers and divers, and the manatees are usually more active at those hours as they forage on the submerged vegetation common to the area. Specific directions to the refuge were provided by a dive shop in Tampa whose owner noted that the turn off of Route 19, into one of the boat rental shops on the bay, was marked prominently by a large billboard advertising, ironically, a housing development.

After winding my way through narrow streets lined by neat rows of Florida ranch homes, I drove into the meandering parking lot of an aged motel complex. Behind the well-worn units, many of which had colorful beach towels draped over the balcony rails, a large scuba shop was nestled on the waters of Kings Bay.

At first glance, it could have been any spot along the Florida coast. Everything had a crowded, used look, as if too many tourists had passed this way before. Spots of black and light green mold blemished the stucco walls of the hotel complex—a common sight resulting from the moist, subtropical air. Small patches of grass that lined the cement walkways were beaten and worn from the tread of too many errant feet. But as I walked toward the scuba shop and caught my first glimpse of the water, I knew I stood at the edge of a different world.

Despite the motel built right to the water's edge, the small marina, and the concrete seawalls protruding into what was once the marshy edge of the bay, the water had a startling iridescent clarity, which gave a wonderful dimensionality to all objects both above and below the surface. Shiny-leafed water hyacinths and silversided mullet, their bright scales glinting in the early morning sun, seemed to float in air. Even the dull, dented aluminum boats took on a dreamy quality as they hovered gracefully above their greenish shadows reflected on the sandy bottom. The water seemed virtually invisible with only a slight turquoise hue hinting at its presence. It was an appropriate setting for meeting creatures from another world.

After changing into a wetsuit, a necessity even in the 74-degree water, I rented a boat and idled out into the area bordering the cordoned-off sanctuary that was marked prominently by white buoys ringing the edge of a small island. After carefully dropping anchor, I loaded the underwater camera, slipped on flippers, mask, and snorkel, and slid quietly into the calm, limpid waters.

In front of me lay a pristine, seemingly ancient watery landscape. Schools of gray snappers darted here and there, boldly approaching but never quite touching my extended hand. Elodea, one of the predominant submerged plants in the estuary, carpeted the reef-like floor, which alternated between depths of a couple of feet to well over a dozen feet. Colorful bluegills, timidly hiding behind grassy ridges, bolted as I kicked into view. Beyond this plethora of marine life I sensed the presence of manatees, hiding somewhere in the crystal blue haze beyond visibility.

When approaching living creatures of great size, such as whales or elephants, I've often felt their presence even before I actually saw them. Perhaps it's more a growing sense of anticipation than any unusual life force emanating from the animals themselves. Yet, it is a distinctive, uncanny feeling which is heightened by both expectation and suspense. I had one of these experiences just before an exciting encounter with a humpback whale a few years ago. I accompanied a friend on a boating trip off the Maine coast to spend a day photographing whales about 25 miles offshore. After some scattered sightings, we settled down to eat a relaxing lunch, enjoying the warm sun and the soft swell that gently rocked the still boat.

I was sitting in a small deck chair on the stern, which was about 2 feet above the water's surface, enjoying my sandwich and making small talk with my host. Suddenly I bolted up out of the chair, turned, and stared into the water immediately off the stern. There was no noise or any disturbance other than a feeling of being watched. And there, just barely submerged off the stern, hovered a large adult humpback, its giant white pectoral fins glowing in the greenish, sunlit waters like the fiery eyes of a demonic aquatic creature from a Jules Verne novel. The silent but distinctive appearance of the curious humpback was a dramatic demonstration of the power of presence.

Swimming now in the waters of Kings Bay, I had the same uncanny feeling. Out there, somewhere very close, swam Florida's mythical mermaids—great, gray leviathans who have visited these waters since long before the coming of man.

As I drifted above the eelgrass, which was swaying gently in the wispy currents of the springs, a movement off to the left caught my eye. There, a huge, shadowy figure moved slowly but purposefully, barely inside the range of visibility. At last, a manatee.

I could hardly contain my excitement as I turned to move toward the giant. The manatee, though, barely seemed to take notice. It was too involved with feeding. Its mouth was stuffed with vegetation, the ends of which drooped limply over the lower lips as the animal chewed its morning meal in a sluggish, indolent manner. The undulating proboscis reminded me of the ample jowls of a fat man feeding contentedly on a huge serving of stringy spaghetti.

The manatee's forelimbs, or flippers, their rounded edges tipped by three miniscule nails, guided the food into its mouth, much like a preschooler learning—but not yet mastering—proper table manners.

I stopped my approach about 10 feet from the animal and studied its bulbous figure. This particular creature was certainly one of the larger adults, probably well over 11 feet in length. Its grayish skin was covered on the dorsal surface by a thin layer of algae which lent a brownish-green cast to the skin tone. Its large spoon-shaped tail was nearly perfect in its symmetry except for an occasional dime-sized nick that gave it an aged, used look.

The face, though, was the most unassuming, nonthreatening one I've ever encountered, defining the manatee's character perfectly. How this animal was ever mistaken for a mermaid says a lot about the psychological condition of sailors who have been at sea too long. Two large lips, sprinkled generously with short, bristly whiskers, dominated a head that seemed to melt into the whole of the gigantic, blubbery body. There was no discernible neck other than an occasional crease that appeared as the animal looked down or to one side or the other. The size of the upper lip made the lower jaw look puny and underslung, giving the manatee a permanent, melancholy frown.

Two deep set eyes, set far apart and to the sides of the head, had the appearance of tiny buttons pushed far into soft, downy material, as if they had been added to the animal's makeup as an afterthought. At the leading edge of the snout were two nostrils, plugged tight by skin valves to prevent water from flooding into the lungs. Looking at the manatee head on, it was easy to imagine that the nostrils were, instead, pressure valves struggling against the intense air pressure of a gigantic gray balloon.

This odd-looking creature, unlike anything I had ever seen before, had characteristics similar to those that had first attracted me to the study of whales. It was a huge, yet remarkably gentle, air-breathing marine mammal. Bizarre in appearance but charmingly attractive; powerful but gentle; once common, now highly endangered. Sadly, its greatest attraction may prove its undoing. As I was to find out, manatees are friendly to a fault.

I kept my distance as the gray behemoth finished its breakfast, obviously not the least distracted by my presence. After five minutes or so in this position, it rotated horizontally, with no discernible effort, until its tail faced me. I took this as a hint and quietly paddled off to explore the rest of the area.

Moments later I happened upon a resting manatee, its snout nestled gently into a patch of soft, sandy bottom. While resting, manatees take on the appearance of giant slugs, their few distinctive features lost in the angle of their posture. While lying on the bottom, this particular animal had both eyes closed, with its flippers pulled tightly to its sides and the tip of its tail tucked slightly under. It stayed in this position for about four or five minutes before opening its eyes, gently arching its back, then rising to the surface for a breath of air—all without ever seeming to move a muscle. After snatching a quick sniff of air, the sleepy giant settled contentedly back on the bottom, once again burying its muzzle into the sand. Apparently manatees, much like whales, get their required amount of rest by taking these "cat naps" from two to twelve hours each day.

I watched it repeat its resting cycle three or four times. The trance-like state of the animal as it floated gently up and down epitomized the perfect relaxation technique and provided an impressive lesson in buoyancy control.

I had been in the water for over an hour already, and the growing chill began to distract my attention from the sleeping manatee. I decided it was time to flex my muscles and move on to explore a little more before the cold brought a halt to my adventure.

Around me the water was alive with fish of all kinds: gray snappers, jacks, schools of mullet, tarpon, and even the pencil-thin needlefish, one of which was always present as if it were my official escort. For several minutes I gamboled about with the multicolored fishes, exploring the plant-covered mounds and crevices that laced the bottom of the bay, stretching my legs and enjoying the freedom of movement, which, because of the striking clarity of the water, made me feel like I was flying. I became so enthralled with the fishes that it took some time before I realized I hadn't seen a manatee for a while.

I stopped to rest my legs for a moment, letting my wetsuit buoy me at the surface. As I gazed into the distance in a relaxed, meditative state, a needlefish startled me by darting from right to left across my facemask. Instinctively, I turned my head to follow, only to find I was mere inches away from the heavily grizzled snout of a very curious adult manatee.

I gave a whoop of surprise through my snorkel and started to quickly backpedal as the huge animal crept toward me in a ghostly, deliberate manner. When something that large is inches away and moving closer still, suddenly the bay didn't seem so big. As it turned out, though, all this guy wanted was a little backscratch. As soon as I reached out and rubbed its ample back, the manatee stopped and hovered in front of me, apparently enjoying the feel of my touch.

Its wrinkled back was covered with a soft algae as well as yellowish encrustations that felt and looked like calloused skin. Judging by the algal growth and the size of the animal, I guessed I was dealing with an old veteran of many winters at Crystal River. I pressed gently as I stroked its back, more to keep my balance than anything else, since the manatee was practically on top of me. Despite its wrinkled, scarred, and mottled look, the skin was remarkably supple and felt like an underinflated inner tube. I continued rubbing and scratching as the giant slowly rolled and exposed its smooth belly to my touch. A moment later, with a minor flick of its tail, it glided out of reach and surfaced for a breath.

It seemed that word got out pretty fast in the manatee community that I was a willing participant in the scratch game as my aged friend was soon joined by a second, smaller manatee. Like two portly but graceful ballet dancers, they pirouetted in front of me in a perfectly choreographed move. Then they glided directly beneath me, chose their moment, and rose under my flippers, lifting me almost completely out of the water. As soon as they drifted out of reach, they'd turn and repeat the maneuver, each time deliberately soliciting contact and all but inviting me to scratch their mottled backs and smooth bellies. This kept up for several minutes until the water was clouded by the silt stirred up by their tails. Then they disappeared as fast as they had come.

By this time, the mid-morning sun was shining down on a growing crowd of snorkelers and divers. The tranquil, pristine waters of the bay were transformed into a chaotic mix of motorized dive platforms, all maneuvering for the best position for their paying customers. Where earlier there had been just over a dozen divers, there were now probably twenty times that number, with more arriving each minute. Eventually, the alarming numbers of people led to confrontation as divers competed with snorkelers for viewing space.

Divers use scuba gear that allows them to remain underwater for extended periods of time, swimming on or close to the bottom as they search for manatees. Unfortunately, the turbulent wake churned up by the motion of their fins often results in a small underwater sand storm as the loose silt is lifted and swirled off the bottom. In addition, the bubbles released from their air tanks often startle and frighten manatees.

Some snorkelers take exception to this type of activity and don't mind saying so. On one occasion I saw a snorkeler dive to the bottom and motion to a diver to surface. When the man obliged and they were both treading water a few feet from me, the snorkeler politely suggested that the diver reconsider the manner in which he was enjoying Kings Bay and its manatees. The diver's reply, however, was not so polite.

Ironically, even with all the heavy recreational use, Crystal River is one area in Florida that has experienced an increase in the manatee population, according to the U.S. Fish & Wildlife Service, which oversees manatee protection programs in the United States and the Caribbean. This is surprising, to say the least. Anyone who has visited Crystal River on a sunny winter weekend can't help but be stunned by the sheer number of human visitors preparing to dive or snorkel with manatees. But here, where the animals are more accessible than anywhere else in Florida, the population thrives. Is it in spite of or because of us?

Part of the reason may be the visible enforcement presence in the area, primarily near the two main sanctuaries at the main spring. Wherever I swam during my visits there, uniformed Marine Patrol officers were nearby in well-marked boats. No doubt there were a few officers posing as divers too. Even so, I did see some overzealous divers chasing manatees, as well as riding on their backs—both actions punishable by stiff fines. But the Marine Patrol can't be everywhere at once, especially in an area as large as Kings Bay, and harassment of manatees continues.

Still, Crystal River remains an ideal winter habitat for manatees. It offers the right depth and temperature and is loaded with the foods manatees prefer; marked sanctuaries provide respite; and ongoing enforcement cuts down on the greatest enemy of these gentle marine mammals: speeding boats. And maybe, just maybe, we can be anthropomorphic enough to believe that manatees truly enjoy our company, the occasional obnoxious visitor notwithstanding.

I took away one significant impression from my first encounter with these gentle creatures: the obvious pleasure they seemed to derive from interacting with people. Curiosity is one thing; enthusiastic congeniality is quite another.

I came to Crystal River with a firm resolve to abide by all the rules. I was not going to approach or try to touch any of the animals—I'd keep my distance so as not to disturb them in their natural habitat. But I forgot to tell the manatees of my plans. Down there they set the rules, and I quickly found out that if they want to use you as a scratching post, you have no say in the matter. On several occasions they literally bowled me over with their interest— not aggressively but certainly deliberately. If I was momentarily distracted by the scenery and not paying attention to the manatees, I'd often turn to find one hovering quietly next to me, much like a pet that feels it is being ignored.

At one point, shortly after the delightful encounter with the two manatees who lifted me out of the water, I found myself in the midst of several exuberant adult manatees swirling in six different directions. It happened suddenly and without warning. At first I was approached by a single animal who slowly presented its belly for me to scratch. As I obliged the first, a second appeared, followed quickly by a third, a fourth, then three or four more. Within the blink of an eye, I found myself engulfed in a turbulent mix of blubbery bodies all vying for attention. Despite their crushing weight and imposing power, I was totally unafraid. As massive and clumsy as they look, they are the epitome of grace and gentleness and rarely bumped me harder than a toddler might nudge a parent. This despite the fact that their antics had stirred up a considerable cloud of silt, which eventually reduced visibility to zero. And again, as quickly as the scene opened, it closed, and they all disappeared into the growing murk.

Finally, the chill of the water had rendered my wetsuit useless, and it was time to go. I had spent the better part of three hours exploring this small part of the intriguing world of the manatee. I came away feeling richer for the experience.

In the iridescent springs of Crystal River, I had discovered a world unlike any other. Take away the human intruders, and what remains is a timeless natural scene filled with all the breathtaking color, beauty, and bizarre creatures found in any fantasy. And, as they have for eons, manatees return each year to this vulnerable environment, blissfully unaware of but not unaffected by the chain of human events. Sadly, theirs is an endangered existence. The recent upsurge of interest in their plight may have come too late to counter decades of indifference.

As I sat in the boat, shivering from the chill of hours spent in the water, I watched the flood of boats and people descending on this fragile scene and wondered.

STRANGE SEA FOLK

Expectations drive the force of imagination. When faced with the unknown, it is often fear mixed with imaginative expectations that creates the demons that haunt our world, whether in dreams or in reality. To stand at the edge of a strange and trackless ocean or upon the bank of a subtropical river on a dark, moonless night can be a sobering experience, even for people who view themselves as fearless. Whatever dangers may lurk beyond the glow of a campfire or a flashlight usually pale against the imagined horrors creeping, slithering, and stalking just outside the line of sight. The familiarity and control that comes with daylight vanishes with the warm rays of the sun, and the explorer is left to the whims of the natural world. It is then that the imagination takes over, and reason may often dissipate.

The feelings of dread that overwhelm most people under such circumstances might be very much like the sensations experienced by the mariners of old as they crossed the boundaries of known science and ventured into distant and exotic lands full of strange and wondrous sights. It is no wonder, then, that accounts of their adventures are filled with imaginative, menacing aquatic beasts.

Reading about the exploits of the early explorers in the comfort and safety of our homes makes it easy to chuckle at the early descriptions and renderings of common sea creatures. Whales are depicted as giant-fanged monsters chewing on caravels and galleons; seals and sea lions take on a hideous, demonic appearance; and octopuses and giant squid suddenly become fanciful, ship-sinking terrors, coiling lengthy tentacles around the masts of ships, hell-bent on the destruction of hapless seafarers. Science has dispelled many of the early myths about the sea and its creatures, but many of the legends live on.

One of the more curious bits of nautical folklore is the comparison between the beautiful, voluptuous mermaid and the chubby manatee and its cousin, the dugong. Practically all literature discussing *Sirenia*, the order of marine mammals that includes manatees and dugongs, mentions the analogy with tongue-in-cheek humor—the blending of myth and reality becomes more understandable in the context of the experiences and expectations of the early mariner.

Despite what most of us learned in grade school, Christopher Columbus did not discover that the world is round—scholars and astronomers had settled on the concept of a spherical globe almost a thousand years before. Even so, the unknown world beyond the horizon still terrified and mystified fifteenth-century mariners, but not enough to dissuade them from seeking the riches many felt could be found in new lands. So they embarked on great voyages of discovery; mapping new routes, discovering new lands, and encountering a variety of unfamiliar creatures, most of which were given fantastic descriptions in the written records of the time. These accounts, coupled with the seaman's penchant for a good story, made it very difficult at that time to tell the difference between fact and fiction.

Since ancient times, the folklore of mermaids has pervaded practically every culture in the world. The names may vary—sirens, nixies, nymphs, silkies, tritons, kelpies, and nereids—but the descriptions remain somewhat similar across cultures and continents. And until the nineteenth century they were actually considered real beasts.

Pliny the Elder, a Roman naturalist from the first century A.D., was the first to describe mermaids in some detail in his monumental work, *Natural History*: "And as for the Meremaids called Nereids, it is no fabulous tale that goeth of them: for looke how painters draw them, so they are indeed: only their bodie is rough and skaled all over, even in those parts wherein they resemble woman." Most mermaids are depicted as half woman, half fish with a sensuous, alluring figure tapering below the waist into the scaly tail of a fish, although some of the sirens of early mythology appear as large birds with the torso and head of a woman. The fishy version is the most enduring, however, and it is here that the similarities with manatees and dugongs begin.

The first account linking the manatee with the mermaid myth in American waters was provided by Columbus on the latter part of his first voyage that began in 1492. When the *Niña* was taking on wood and water in Northern Hispaniola (the present-day Dominican Republic), he sent a small boat to explore the lower course of the Rio Yaque del Norte, a river which flowed into the Atlantic not too far from his ship's anchorage. Columbus notes in his journal that while reconnoitering the river one of his men "saw three *serenas* who rose very high from the sea, but they were not as beautiful as they are painted, although to some extent they have a human appearance in the face. He said that he had seen some in Guinea on the coast of Malagueta." This last reference proves that at least one of Columbus' crew had previously sighted West African manatees while on the coast of that great continent, prior to the explorations of the New World.

It is not difficult to imagine what went through the minds of the superstitious seamen aboard the ship's boat when the manatees first stuck their grizzled snouts above the river's surface. If indeed they thought they were sighting mermaids, their fear must have been intense. Despite their partially human form, mermaids were believed to be soulless, pitiless creatures whose beguiling beauty lured seamen to the depths of the ocean for it was only by marrying mortals that mermaids could acquire a soul. In the fifteenth century, mermaids had come to symbolize the abduction of the Christian soul and were used as church symbols, appearing on carved pews and church pillars. For the devout Christians who sailed with Columbus, the appearance of the manatees may have been perceived as a test of their faith. Although it seems quite a stretch to equate the rotund, almost featureless manatee to a smooth-skinned enchantress with long flowing tresses and alluring eyes, it is important to remember that centuries ago mermaids were also believed to be able to assume many shapes, from a charming creature like the Little Mermaid of Disney's movie, to terrifying monsters with pointed teeth and snake-like bodies.

Some anthropologists, naturalists, and folklorists believe that dugongs and not manatees may have been the origin of the mermaid myth, which dates back long before written history. Dugongs range over a wide area of the Indo-Pacific, from Australia and the Indian Ocean to the Red Sea. For the ancient cultures that bordered on these waters, the dugong must have been a familiar animal whose folkloric persona wound its way through many cultures and centuries eventually to pervade all maritime folklore. Representative embellishments of the varied cultures combined to form the images we know today.

The tie between dugongs and mermaids is clear even as recently as the eighteenth century. In one set of natural history volumes published in the early 1700s, a description of the so-called Amboine Mermaid sounds a lot like a young dugong:

A monster resembling a Siren caught near the island of Borne in the Department of Amboine. It was 59 inches long and in proportion as an eel. It lived on land for four days and seven hours in a vat full of water. From time to time it uttered little cries like those of a mouse. Although offered small fish, shells, crabs, lobsters, etc., it would not eat. After its death some excreta, like that of a cat, was found in its barrel.

The size and smooth, eel-like shape of the Amboine creature would fit that of a young dugong, which could presumably survive for a few days in a large tub of water. Since dugongs do emit short whistling sounds—or in the case of a calf, bleating sounds like those of a lamb—the description of the cries would be appropriate. In fact, Australian aborigines called some dugongs *whistlers* for the sound they made. And since dugongs are herbivores, none of the foodstuffs offered would have interested the poor creature.

In 1732, a more detailed description of a captured mermaid comes from the French priest Père Labat in his translation of a book on Africa written by an Italian named Cavazzi who wrote of a *fish-woman* he encountered in a West African river:

> Its face is as ugly as its name is beautiful, if one can call it a face at all. Its mouth—or rather its snout—is incredibly wide, has cleft lips and veritable tusks. The bulging eyes protrude from the sockets, the nose looks as though it had been squashed. Two heavy breasts hang down over its bristly belly. It has two arms and five three-jointed fingers on each hand, but the fingers are joined together by a strong, pliable web as in ducks. From the waist down the creature is a fish with a forked tail. Its thick stringy skin is so elastic that it can hide its young therein as in a cloak. The negroes eat its blubbery, almost indigestible flesh.

This is an almost perfect description of a female dugong (*Dugong dugon*), with the exception of the bulging eyes and elastic skin, both of which could have been present in a dead dugong if Cavazzi's animal had been captured and killed by the natives. The snout, tusks, breasts (actually large teats located beneath the pectoral fins in approximately the same area as a woman's breasts), bristly belly, pectoral fins (which could appear as joined fingers to individuals unfamiliar with the animal), and forked tail are all physical characteristics of a dugong. Also, Africans do hunt both manatees and dugongs for food. The only major discrepancy in this account is the location of the sighting. Manatees, which have horizontal spoon-shaped tails and no tusks, are common to rivers in West Africa, while dugongs are found in small numbers in marine habitats on the East African coast. Perhaps, however, the true location of Cavazzi's mermaid was lost in the translation of the original document.

As recently as the twentieth century, one freighter captain mistook several dugongs for shipwreck survivors. As his freighter moved through the Red Sea in 1905, the captain thought he saw three people swimming with their chests out of water far offshore. He slowed the ship, signalled, and approached them. The captain was surprised to find that the "survivors" were actually dugongs, who looked on and then dove.

Another irony of the mermaid legend is that while everyone is familiar with the mythological creature, few people are capable of identifying the unusual animals that may have been the origin of the myth. It has been the fate of both manatees and dugongs to live in relative obscurity, known only to those who live in the regions where they are common, although their status as endangered mammals and a growing environmental awareness has increased their visibility in the past few decades. Still, they remain remarkably enigmatic creatures for most people, despite increasing media coverage.

I can think of several personal recollections that prove my point. For example, I recently visited Blue Spring State Park in

Orange City, Florida, to observe the manatees that seek the warmth of Blue Spring Run in the winter. Extending over one section of the run is an observation platform built by the Florida Department of Natural Resources. It provides an excellent vantage point for viewing not only manatees but the scores of fish that swim in the clear and shallow spring waters directly below the platform pilings. As I stood there photographing several manatees resting not 30 feet from the platform, I was amused to overhear one gentleman expounding at great length about the manatee he was pointing out for his interested listeners. They looked on in respectful silence with only an occasional nod or gasp punctuating his extended natural history lesson which touched on the great size of manatees and their endangered status. Unfortunately, his "manatee" was in fact a longnose gar fish, which swam to and fro, totally unaware of its elevated status as a marine mammal. Although the longnose gar is indeed large, maybe two or three feet in length, its dark body and needlenose snout bear hardly any resemblance to a manatee. Yet this group didn't need any convincing.

On another occasion at the same location, I accompanied Ranger Wayne Hartley as he canoed the run, taking his morning count of the manatees on hand that day. So far he had counted up to thirty-seven manatees, many of which were lazily snoozing or moving about below our canoe. As we passed within 20 feet of the platform, which hangs a good 8 feet up over the water, one of the visitors standing nearby shouted, "Are there any manatees in today?" Since the water there is almost as clear as air and many of the manatees that were cavorting around us were well over 10 feet in length, I concluded that knowing what to look for is half the battle. The truth is, they're just not as familiar to most people as land animals or other marine mammals their size.

As for dugongs, most people greet me with a blank stare when I ask if they know about the animal. But then it is not found in this part of the world. On the other hand, Australia is a prime habitat of dugongs. Nevertheless, when I called the Australian Embassy in Washington, DC, to request some scientific studies on dugongs, the embassy librarian, a native Australian, had never even heard of the creature. However, she did eventually send some good information gleaned from her sources there.

Not long ago, my wife and I had an opportunity to entertain a couple who had just moved to Canada from northwestern Australia. They were visiting close friends of ours around the holidays, so we were pleased to extend an invitation to them and their children to join us for a New Year's Day luncheon. When I found out what part of Australia they had lived in, apparently not far from Shark Bay, where one of the largest populations of dugongs live, I couldn't wait to ask them how many dugongs they had seen and if they had any stories to share. Sadly, they hadn't heard of the animal either.

These are isolated incidents and not scientific studies, but they have convinced me that few people are aware of these fascinating, mysterious, and docile creatures—some of the more unusual species of mammals that share this satellite of air, land, and water called Earth. To miss their story is to miss a remarkable piece of the puzzle of life.

The West Indian manatee, the primary focus of this book, is one of only four living species in the warm-blooded, air-breathing mammalian order of *Sirenia*, which is named after the mythological sirens first reported by early mariners. A fifth and much larger species, Steller's sea cow (*Hydrodamalis gigas*), was hunted to extinction within twenty-seven years of its discovery off two small islands in a remote part of the Bering Sea in 1741. Stellar's sea cow was unique because of its great size, estimated at up to 26 feet, and because it was the only species of *Sirenia* that lived in cold water and fed exclusively on marine algae.

The living sirens, consisting of three species of manatees and one species of dugong, are the only wholly herbivorous (plant-eating) marine mammals, and all are subtropical or tropical in distribution. The West Indian manatee (*Trichechus manatus*) inhabits shallow coastal waters, rivers, and springs of extreme southeastern North America, through the Caribbean and down to northeastern South America. The animals found in Florida are a subspecies of West Indian manatee and are usually referred to as Florida manatees (*Trichechus manatus latinostris*). The West African manatee (*Trichechus senegalensis*) is found in the coastal waters and rivers of western Africa and is very similar in looks and behavior to its West Indian counterpart. The Amazonian manatee (*Trichechus inunguis*), however, is restricted to the fresh waters on the upper and central courses of the rivers in the Orinoco and Amazon systems and does not have the nails found on the edge of the flippers of the West Indian and West African species. It is the smallest of the living manatees, with the longest recorded specimen measuring just over 9 feet in length. The dugong (*Dugon dugon*) is widely distributed throughout the Indian and Pacific oceans, including the Persian Gulf and the Red Sea, with the largest known populations in northern Australian waters. Sadly, all four species are endangered.

Sirenians evolved from four-footed land mammals about 55 million years ago. Blood protein analysis and fossil evidence relates them to present-day elephants and rabbit-sized plant eating African and Asian mammals known as hyraxes. Through evolution, sirenians have lost most of their hair but retain small vestigial pelvic bones as evidence of their terrestrial beginnings. They breed, calve, and suckle in water and are unable to emerge onto land although some manatees have been seen heaving the forward part of their bodies up onto riverbanks to get at choice vegetation.

All sirenians, commonly called *sea cows* because of their cattle-like docility and herbivorous diet, are large and cylindrically shaped, with significant blubber stores that give them a rotund, balloon-like appearance. The front limbs have been modified into flippers with the skeletal structure of a five-fingered hand, but vestigial nails exist in only the West Indian and the West African manatee. These pectoral-fin nails look very much like the toenails of elephants.

Even though dugongs resemble manatees in many ways, they are considered to be more specialized. While manatees utilize salt- and fresh-water habitats, the dugong is strictly a marine, or salt-water, dweller. With a horizontal, whale-like tail, shorter and less mobile flippers, and a slimmer, more streamlined body, the dugong is a more efficient swimmer than the manatee, which doesn't need as much swimming efficiency and endurance simply because it is less active and inhabits more protected waters. While the muscle systems are very similar in the two species, the shoulder muscles are quite different, perhaps reflecting the requirements of maneuvering in a more turbulent, open habitat as compared to the protected habitats of manatees.

One of the more curious features specific to manatees is their mode of tooth replacement. Most mammals, including humans, start with so-called milk teeth which are later shed to accommodate permanent, adult teeth. Manatees, however, have molars that erupt in the back of the jaw and migrate forward, replacing from twenty to thirty teeth per jaw throughout most of the animal's lifetime. The old teeth, worn smooth by a diet of abrasive plants often mixed with sand, fall out the front, allowing the back molars to move forward, a process that constantly renews the grinding surface. This unusual characteristic was studied in detail by a group of researchers led by paleontologist Dr. Daryl Domning, who was doing research on captive Amazonian manatees at the National Institute of Amazonian Research in Manaus, Brazil, in 1975. Since the research facility did not have the budget to support large oceanarium-style tanks with sophisticated filtering systems, manatees were kept in prefabricated plastic swimming pools, which had to be drained and cleaned by hand each week. In the early part of the study, a research student cleaning one of the pools found a single manatee tooth on the bottom. Over the next several years a total of sixty-six teeth from seven manatees were found, allowing Domning and Lee-Ann Hayek, of the Smithsonian Institution, to measure the rate of tooth replacement and its relation to the manatee diet. While they found that tooth wear is caused by the grinding of abrasive particles, tooth movement is stimulated by chewing. The tougher and more fibrous the plant material eaten, the faster the teeth fall out.

It may seem hard to believe, but the development of this kind of teeth has had an effect on the distribution of manatees and dugongs, at least in the New World. Fossil records indicate that both animals were once found in this region, but manatees prevailed because they evolved more wear-resistant teeth, allowing them to exploit developing areas of fresh-water vegetation.

Dugong dentition is very different from that of manatees and consists mostly of a few ever-growing molars that are continually worn down by the constant chewing of sea grasses, resulting in smooth peg-like structures. Male and female dugongs have small tusks, but they are usually visible only in older females and in males starting at about twelve to fifteen years of age. These tusks are minor compared to those found on their distant cousin, the elephant, since they usually erupt only an inch or so above the gum line.

Among living sirenians, the West Indian manatee is the largest species with individuals exceeding 12 feet in length and weighing over 3,500 pounds, although these sizes represent the extreme upper limit of growth. The average manatee is just under 10 feet long and weighs anywhere from 800 to 1,200 pounds. By comparison, the maximum length of a dugong can exceed 11 feet, with an upper weight limit of about 2,000 pounds. The average size of a dugong, though, is closer to 9 feet and 1,000 pounds.

Their statistics, while impressive, are not what make sirenians unique. They are, quite simply, unusual by their existence, an anachronism in a fast-paced world where power speaks and overt aggression is a universal characteristic. Sirenians represent the opposite end of the scale—simple, gentle mammals whose nonthreatening nature and slow-paced lifestyle put them at risk for survival. While frenetic events convulse the terrestrial world, casting an ever-longer shadow on life beneath the sea, sirenians maintain a docile lifestyle refined by millions of years of evolution, unchanged in many ways since before the age of man.

Although man's exploitation of these animals can be measured in centuries, we actually know very little about them. What has been learned comes from studies, conducted over the past few decades, that are only beginning to shed light on the evolution, habitat, physiology, and behavior of these creatures. In many ways, they are still very much an enigma—spectral leviathans existing on the coastal fringes of humanity—admired, loved, ignored by many, understood by few.

The name *manati* is believed to be a Spanish adoption of *manattoui*, the name for manatees used by the Caribs of the West Indies at the time of the early explorers. The Dutch and English called manatees "sea cows" because they closely resembled the terrestrial mammals in habit, diet, and flavor. As early as 1594, the French used the term *lamentin*, which, according to Captain C. M. Scannon, alluded to the sea cow's lamentations upon seeing its calf killed. The scientific name *Sirenia* was assigned to the order by a nineteenth-century taxonomist who may have been familiar with Columbus' first reference to the animals.

The seemingly uncomplicated behavior of manatees is actually well-suited to their needs and reflects millions of years of adaptation to a specific environment. Since they evolved in habitats where food was plentiful and temperatures constant, manatees did not develop the complex behaviors found in other animal species. This lack of environmental stress has led them to develop relatively unstructured social lives with no daily routines. They feed, rest, and play anytime, day or night, although some activities, including feeding, may be regulated by winter air temperatures. In this case, they conserve energy as much as possible, resting until the springs are warmest, then leaving to feed.

Manatees spend six to eight hours each day grazing on submerged, emergent, and floating vegetation, including a variety of sea grasses and fresh-water plants, consuming up to 11 percent of their body weight each day. Some of their favorite foods include various sea grasses and plants such as manatee, turtle, or shoal grasses and wild celery, water milfoil, and water hyacinths. Using their remarkably flexible upper lips, they grasp and crop the food, forcing it back to the grinding molars where it is thoroughly chewed. Their digestive systems are well adapted to processing the large amounts of high-fiber low-protein food needed to maintain their substantial body weight. To augment their diet, manatees often dig up grasses with their flippers to get at the roots, where much of the biomass and carbohydrates are concentrated.

A manatee feeding on water hyacinths looks very much like a polite but gluttonous human. It approaches the floating plant from below with its head and back slightly awash. Gently grasping the plant with its projected lips, the manatee pulls it below and begins delicately nibbling at the juicy leaves, holding the hyacinth in front of its mouth with the tip of its flippers and masticating its food with great facial movements. Usually it eats only the leaves, drops the stalk and roots, then grabs a fresh hyacinth to continue its meal.

During the winter, manatees need a large amount of food, each day consuming about a pound of food for every 10 pounds of body weight and storing the energy required to maintain body heat in colder water. When the weather gets particularly cold, manatees become relatively inactive and may even fast, minimizing movement to maintain energy stores. Observers at Blue Spring noted that several manatees there did not feed for over a week during a cold spell. When aquatic vegetation becomes somewhat sparse during the early winter, manatees have been observed munching on acorns that have fallen from overhanging live oak trees. Captive manatees have been fed a remarkable variety of foods, from lawn grass, bread, palmetto fronds, and fruit to fish and meat, indicating that they are opportunistic feeders with a varied diet.

One of the mysteries about their lifestyle concerns their need for fresh water. Living and feeding in both fresh and salt water presumably places some pressure on their water-balance mechanisms, but biologists still aren't sure whether they require fresh water to survive. Explorer William Dampier first brought the question to light in 1681 when he wrote, "Manatees that live in the sea do commonly come once or twice in twenty-four hours to the mouth of any freshwater river that is near their place of abode." Nowadays, numerous observers have seen manatees drinking fresh water from hoses hanging off of piers as well as from culverts and sewage outfalls in saline areas. This apparent need for fresh water may make them even more vulnerable to entrapment or pollution since it may bring them into closer contact with people and their manufactured environment. There is plenty of evidence to indicate that manatees are sensitive to human intrusion. For example, they often feed at the edge of sea-grass beds, presumably because the nearby deep water provides them with an easy escape route if disturbed. When harassed or frightened, a manatee's only defense is to swim away. They seem incapable of aggressive behavior. On numerous occasions, I have seen manatees simply turn and swim away from divers or snorkelers whose zealous behavior would entice most wild animals to attack.

Despite their great size, manatees are fluid, graceful animals with great agility underwater. By changing the volume of air in their lungs through relaxation or muscular contractions, manatees move effortlessly, seemingly unaware of up or down. One of the factors contributing to this neutral buoyancy is their extremely dense bones, which lack marrow cavities in the ribs and long bones of the forelimbs. This bone density increases specific gravity—the fewer air pockets in the bones, the more control—allowing manatees to move vertically without apparent effort. I have found this to be one of their most fascinating traits. To watch a manatee glide upside down or perform rolls, somersaults, head and tail stands is akin to watching an underwater ballet, so fluid and effortless are the motions. Although they generally move very slowly—about 2 to 6 miles per hour—they are capable of short bursts of speed exceeding 15 miles per hour in order to elude pesky pursuers.

Speed, however, is not the most obvious manatee trait. Resting seems to be their preferred habit. On one of my first winter visits to Blue Spring, I spent hours watching manatees rest, most of them snuggled snout-first into the sandy bottom, rising every three to four minutes to catch a breath. In this posture, they bear a great resemblance to giant gray slugs, actually spending up to twelve hours a day snoozing on the bottom. While resting, a large manatee can stay submerged for up to twenty minutes before rising for a breath of air. When I snorkel near manatees resting in Crystal River, I observed that they seemed totally oblivious to any nearby activity, unless disturbed by a direct touch. In these trance-like states, they must have indeed been easy prey for hunters.

Although manatees spend most of their time resting and feeding, they also exhibit behaviors that could be defined as play. On numerous occasions I've watched them frolic with seemingly wild abandon, at times bolting and turning, grasping each other with pectoral fins, leaping partly out of the water, mouthing flukes and backs, and even kissing muzzle to muzzle. Kissing, an endearing behavior that looks particularly human, may actually be a form of greeting to assist in individual recognition. Daniel S. Hartman, whose landmark study of West Indian manatees at Crystal River in the late 1960s remains the most comprehensive collection of information available on these animals, noted that play usually occurred only when the manatees were well rested, fed, and free of human harrassment.

Although essentially solitary animals, manatees are also fairly social, gathering in temporary groups without regard to age, sex, or territory. An example of this is the groups of young males, too young to mate, that temporarily gather in the presence of an estrous female. Other examples are the strong association between a cow and her calf which can last up to two years, representing the only true manatee family unit and the mating herd, a group consisting of a cow pursued by courting bulls. During this time, a female will attempt to avoid the interests of the males as they jostle for a favorable position, sometimes almost stranding herself in shallow water. When the female is receptive, copulation occurs with one or more bulls abdomen-to-abdomen with the male below.

Manatees breed year-round and calve throughout the year. However, their slow reproductive rate is one of the primary reasons they are endangered. Females, who are capable of producing a calf every three to five years, are ready for reproduction at seven to eight years of age; males at about nine or ten. Gestation lasts about thirteen months with each pregnancy producing a single calf, although twins are possible. Newborns, which are about 4 feet long and weigh just over 60 pounds, remain dependent on their mothers for up to two years, nursing underwater from teats located at the base of the cow's pectoral fins. Calves latch on for up to three minutes at a time to consume milk rich in fats, proteins, and salt.

The bond between cow and calf is strong, with the mother acting as teacher as well as the primary food supply for the first few months. One captive female was seen with her calf on her back, holding it above water for 45 minutes and dunking it repeatedly to establish its breathing rhythm. New research also suggests that cows and their young may recognize and stay close to each other for many years after weaning, enabling the mother to teach migration routes and the locations of feeding grounds and winter refuges. For tropical animals that live in a wide-ranging area in a subtropical environment, knowledge of migration routes and winter refuges is key to survival.

Although Florida is the northernmost end of their year-round range, Florida manatees are occasionally reported as far north as Virginia and as far west as Texas. In the summer, they are usually found in small groups throughout the waters of coastal Florida. In the winter, when air temperatures drop below 50 degrees and water temperatures drop below about 60 degrees, they congregate in larger groups at warm-water refuges. Those that fail to make the trip south before the onset of winter probably do not survive.

Historically, the winter range of manatees was centered in southern Florida with only small groups going to warm-water springs in northern Florida. However, loss of habitat and the construction of power plants, with their warm-water effluents, over the past three decades has caused a shift in the distribution of manatees during the winter, making utilities such as Florida Power & Light unwilling, though responsible, seasonal caretakers of large populations of these endangered mammals.

Manatees are capable of traveling tremendous distances to migrate with the seasons. One animal was reported to have traveled over 528 miles between Blue Spring on the St. John's River and Coral Gables to the south. Another manatee took only four days to swim 143 miles from the Indian River in Florida to southern

Georgia. One of the ways biologists are able to gather information on the seasonal movements of manatees is through the use of radio-tracking devices, which allows them to unravel many of the mysteries involving the dispersal of manatees in the summer months.

Compared to manatees, dugongs are at best enigmatic creatures. On a scale of one to ten, with ten representing the scientific community's complete familiarity with an animal's physiology, biology, and ecology, manatees might rate a four, dugongs a one. The easiest way to elicit a puzzled look from someone is to ask them to describe a dugong. Most people are comfortably familiar with many large marine mammals, primarily whales, dolphins, and seals, but few have ever heard of a dugong. This may be due to several factors, ranging from its Indo-Pacific distribution to its shy and elusive behavior.

The renowned French author, Jules Verne, however, gave the dugong some exposure in popular fiction in his renowned novel of 1875, *The Mysterious Island*, although the treatment of the animal's character was somewhat less than accurate. In the story, several men and a trusty dog escape in a hot air balloon from a prisoner of war camp during the Civil War. While aloft they get caught in a violent storm and are carried far off course to the mysterious island, located somewhere out in the Pacific. While reconnoitering a lake found on the island, the dog suddenly becomes very agitated, plunges into the lake, and starts swimming toward a disturbance some distance offshore. Suddenly a huge head "with large eyes, and adorned with long silky mustaches" emerges from the water.

At first the men call it a *lamentin*, the French term for manatee; but Verne, as the narrator, describes it instead as the dugong which, he writes, is "one of that species of the order of cetaceans."

The dugong attacks the dog and drags it underwater where a tremendous struggle ensues as the men stand by helplessly.

Within moments, the dog is thrown 10 feet above the surface, drops back into the agitated water, then escapes to shore. The dugong is mysteriously killed underwater while battling the dog, eventually washing up on the lake shore. Verne describes "the formidable dugong" as "fifteen or sixteen feet long" and weighing "from three to four thousand pounds." Eventually the story's characters use the animal's flesh for food, noting that "in the islands of the Malay Archipelago and elsewhere, it is especially reserved for the table of native princes."

For many people at the turn of the century, this brief depiction of the dugong may have been their only exposure to the animal. Verne undoubtedly thought the animal was exotic enough to include in a book about an island filled with unusual creatures, although his description incorrectly classifies the dugong as a cetacean, or whale, and in no way represents the true nature of the animal.

The name *dugong* is Malaysian in origin and is used to identify this species of *Sirenia* throughout Asia, Japan, and the southwest Pacific. In fact, the Chinese have a written character that is pronounced "dugong." This distant cousin of the manatee does not inhabit lakes (as Verne wrote in his book) but tropical and subtropical shallow coastal waters with yearly water temperatures ranging from 68 to 91 degrees Fahrenheit. Its range encompasses almost the entire coast of the Indian Ocean: from east Africa north to the Red Sea; around the southern Asian coast to the South China Sea and south to the Philippines, Borneo, and New Guinea; down to the north coast of Australia. Throughout almost all of this vast range the dugong is endangered and may have already disappeared in many parts. The largest population, estimated at around ten thousand animals, lives in Shark Bay in northwestern Australia, where most of the studies of this shy creature have been focused.

Despite their similarity in size, shape, and coloring to manatees, dugongs have specific features that set them apart from the rest of the living *Sirenia*. At first glance their whale-like tails give them the appearance of chubby dolphins. Compared to manatees their bodies are much more streamlined, an adaptation that helps them maneuver in a more exposed marine environment, with shorter and less mobile pectoral fins missing the familiar nails found on Florida manatees. Their thick, slate-gray skin is much smoother than that of a manatee and is covered by sparse, short hairs which become very dense on the muzzle and around the mouth, itself a complex and versatile structure. The most prominent part of their muzzle is a flattened facial disk, somewhat like a horseshoe in shape and oriented ventrally, which can be manipulated to grasp plant material and convey it to the mouth, much like the tip of an elephant's trunk. In another striking similarity to their terrestrial relatives, dugong adult males, and some older females, have very short tusks hidden behind the disk, which, because of their size, are not considered formidable weapons.

Like the manatee, dugongs have no discernible neck, although they can move their heads up and down and side to side to a limited extent, which helps them as they forage on sea grasses found in vast meadows in intertidal and subtidal zones. Again showing similarities to elephants, dugongs prefer to rid their food of sand and silt and will grab a mouthful of plants and shake it vigorously in an apparent effort to avoid ingesting too much grit. They have also been observed piling plants into small stacks, allowing time for sandy particles and small marine creatures to settle out and returning to consume the stack of food later.

Dugongs prefer to feed at night, hence their nickname *moon creatures*, and will spend the daylight hours swimming offshore. This may be an adaptation to hunting pressures or, as some scientists believe, may indicate a preference for feeding with the rising tide and following it out on the ebb. This is one of the reasons they remain largely enigmatic creatures. Much of what is known about dugongs is extrapolated from the study of manatees, specifically the Florida manatee, and efforts are underway to unravel firsthand many of the mysteries still surrounding these unusual mammals. But what we already know adds up to a fascinating picture of an animal perfectly adapted to its shallow coastal marine environment.

For example, a dugong's bones are so dense they act like natural weight belts, helping dugongs overcome buoyancy problems as they bottom feed in salt water. The thick bones of their ribs, so dense they were once prized as ivory by native hunters, have developed to protect their sensitive internal organs from attacks by sharks and other large marine carnivores. Interestingly, the skin is thickest dorsally, or on the uppermost portion of their backs. This adaptation of the ribs and dorsal skin is perfect for a bottom-feeding creature whose greatest threat is an attack from above.

A dugong's blubber layer is much thinner than that of most other marine mammals, reflecting a special adaptation to a warm-water environment. In addition, its snout, as mentioned earlier, is oriented more toward the bottom than a manatee's—this because dugongs rarely, if ever, feed on floating surface vegetation like other Sirenia. Unlike manatees, dugongs appear to be physiologically independent of fresh water, which makes a lot of sense for a creature that spends its life in salt water.

Although they bear many similarities to manatees behaviorally, as in the cow-calf bond, for example, recent research dispels the previously held belief that dugongs are gentle giants.

A noted expert on the dugong, biologist Paul K. Anderson of the University of Calgary in Alberta, Canada, recently discovered that males are territorial and engage in violent combat for breeding rights to an estrous female. Males will vigorously defend barren pieces of territory called *leks* in the hopes of attracting interested females who intrude on the territory only to mate. Manatees, on the other hand, have never shown any inclination to set up or defend territories, although, as previously mentioned, they do get involved in boisterous behavior while pursuing an estrous female.

Unfortunately, like manatees, dugongs have very slow reproductive rates, with a female producing a calf every three to five years after gestation periods of thirteen to fourteen months. Their prereproductive period is nine to ten years for both sexes. So in spite of their longevity, which, like manatees, is estimated at seventy years depending on the source of information, dugongs remain endangered throughout most of their range, with Australia being the only location where populations seem stable or possibly on the increase.

Despite the advances in the study of dugongs over the past few years, in some ways they remain a creature enshrouded in myth for those in the more primitive cultures of the Pacific region.

In the late 1970s, while involved in anthropological fieldwork with the Barok natives of New Ireland, an island province of Papua, New Guinea, Roy Wagner, an American cultural anthropologist, was intrigued by reports of a marine mammal the natives called the *Ri* or *Ilkai*, which they believed to be a semi-human creature, much like the mermaid of Western art and folklore.

In 1983 Dr. Wagner organized a small expedition to explore the possibility that it might be a new species of marine mammal. After interviewing native fishermen, the team was successful in locating the animal and enjoyed brief but inconclusive sightings in Nokon Bay in the southern portion of New Ireland. What they saw convinced the scientists that the animal was indeed a marine mammal, although its ten-minute dive time and pronounced vertical flexion seemed to eliminate the possibility that it was a dugong.

Two years later, a second, more ambitious expedition was launched to the same bay, this time accompanied by divers and a video crew. On their arrival, they immediately sighted the animal some distance away. At the same time, a local villager approached the dive boat in a rowboat, pointed at the animal, and proclaimed it was an *Ilkai*, the female member of a family consisting of a family including a male and a child that lived in the bay. He told the expedition members that the female had a woman's face, hair, hands, and breasts.

Shortly afterward, the captain of the dive boat sighted the creature while snorkeling in the same vicinity. His description matched perfectly that of a dugong. Three days later, suspicions were confirmed tragically when several villagers were observed pulling a dead female dugong up onto the beach. The animal had been killed by a single gunshot wound from a high-powered rifle.

For the natives of Nokon Bay, and for the expedition members who had traveled thousands of miles in the hopes of shedding the light of science into a distant corner of the world, it was a brutal end to a beautiful myth. What lay on the sand before them was no alluring siren of the deep, no beguiling enchantress, simply a bloodied dugong, its myth laid bare, its life extinguished. Perhaps now the magic is gone for these islanders, their charming legend of the mermaid nothing more than a thousand-pound mammal pulled unceremoniously onto their beach. But they, like all of us, must look beyond our expectations and dreams to realize that the real enchantress is nature and its diversity of wildlife. To do so is in itself a revelation. For we may not be able to ensure that our myths will last forever, but there is much we can do to ensure that nature, in all its varied and colorful forms, remains to charm us with its mystery.

FACES IN THE CROWD

This was a most disconcerting moment. I had a quick decision to make. Do I or do I not dance with this stranger? Like a teenager approached by a new suitor at a high school dance, I was confronted with the inevitability of making a momentary decision. Not that I shy away from making choices, mind you. It's just that the usual criteria for choosing a dance partner didn't apply in this instance. She (I use the term without a great degree of confidence) weighed several hundred pounds, had a face like a large gray pincushion, skin like a calloused inner tube, a body shaped like a large Maine potato, was as bald as billiard ball, had no legs to speak of, and could have been a male rather than female.

I usually don't have trouble distinguishing between the sexes, but this particular stranger was different. Very different. This was the most aggressively friendly manatee I had ever encountered and, like the sirens of ancient mythology, it was using all the guile it could muster to lure me into a whirling dance every bit as graceful and fluid as an underwater ballet.

My amorous friend—let's refer to it as "she" just to keep my male ego intact—was literally all over me. I couldn't get away if I wanted to. As my wife, Kathy, looked on with bemused fascination, not the slightest hint of jealousy showing through her facemask, my big gray suitor spun and rolled in the water around me, rubbing first its back then its belly against my wetsuit, arching in ever closer circles until I could barely move. I was getting claustrophobic, and the manatee seemed to be getting excited. Carefully, I watched her tiny eye as it moved to follow me.

At times the stare was direct, at other times it was distant, much like the glazed, squinty look of a man with poor vision. This youngster was clearly as farsighted as its brethren, a characteristic of manatees that results in a humorous tendency to bump into objects that fall outside their range of focus. Touch seems to be far more important to manatees than sight, hence their preference for a high amount of body contact. Perhaps this explains why my friend was using me as a scratching post, although these nudges were definitely more than blind blunderings or unintentional bumps.

My adventure with the flirtatious manatee had its beginnings several weeks before when I called my close friend and former college roommate, Glenn DuPont. Glenn was now a successful dentist in St. Petersburg. His wife, Janet, and four young daughters were to accompany Kathy and me and our two little girls, Lani and Erin, on a snorkeling trip to Crystal River. Glenn and I had both snorkeled at Crystal River before, and we wanted to introduce our families to manatees firsthand, to give them an opportunity to view this particular marine world and its unique creatures. We solidified our plans on the phone, deciding to rent a large pontoon boat to carry our substantial brood out onto the waters of Kings Bay in mid-January, weather permitting.

When the day arrived the weather was perfect—sunny and just cool enough to entice the manatees to gather near the main spring off the south side of Banana Island. After preparing the boat and outfitting the crew—stuffing six girls, ranging in age from four to thirteen, into wetsuits takes some time—we got underway around mid-morning. Within moments we were gently dropping anchor near the main spring, an act that plunged our young crew into a frantic scramble for facemasks and flippers. One by one we eased into the water fanning out in several directions, buoyed by high spirits and neoprene wetsuits, searching for our first glimpse of Crystal River's most famous residents.

Visibility was moderate, maybe 10 to 15 feet, so everything we saw appeared abruptly, without warning, adding to the tense excitement. A large school of sleek, colorful tarpon bolted out of the greenish haze ahead, setting off a watery stampede of splashing, sputtering girls, gasping noisily as they fought for breath in their agitation. For children accustomed to viewing large fish on the other side of the tank or from topside in a boat, this was a heady experience. Tarpon look a lot larger in their own world than when viewed from ours. When you're a child, dwarfed by many of the creatures in the water around you, their impact is certainly heightened. The tarpon, however, were gone as fast as they appeared, melting like wispy phantoms into the turquoise haze behind us and allowing calm to once again settle on this intrepid group of explorers.

As we swam along the outside edge of the roped-off sanctuary, heading for an area near the main spring, visibility worsened until we could barely see 5 or 6 feet ahead. Lani, and now Catherine, one of Glenn's daughters, clung tightly to my hands as we sallied forth into the gloom, straining our eyes for any sign of something big and gray. Their growing apprehension was evident in the increased drag as they ceased their kicking, preferring instead to have me pull them into an experience they weren't too confident they were going to enjoy. The prickly pear snout of a manatee took shape directly in front of us without any warning whatsoever, sending both my young colleagues into a terror-stricken frenzy that made the tarpon sighting pale by comparison.

I've never considered manatees to be very intimidating creatures. In fact they've always reminded me of the formless *shmoos* from the *Li'l Abner* comic strip. But their size can be imtimidating at first, especially for two young girls who had expected creatures rather like the stuffed animals at home. Splashing, thrashing, and screeching, Lani and Catherine battled gamely for space on the top of my head that still managed to stay above water.

Fortunately, all the ruckus sent the manatee in the opposite direction, so a fragile calm finally prevailed once the girls realized that nothing in its right mind would have stuck around after that theatrical display.

It was later in the day that Kathy and I met up with the flirtatious manatee. It started out like every other encounter that day—a slow approach followed by a couple of casual passes to solicit a scratch. Catherine had rejoined us after lunch, her nerves now steeled by several sightings. She swam behind me, just off my shoulder, as the young manatee kept up its advances. Judging by its small size and comical, bulbous figure, and the large adult that hovered nearby the whole time, I guessed it was a nursing calf. I knew from experience that this was going to get very interesting.

With manatee calves, like the whale calves I had grown familiar with over the years, it's best to expect the unexpected. Whales that have grown up with the whale-watching industry often show no fear or hesitation in approaching boats and will solicit contact in creative and unusual ways. One particular humpback in the Gulf of Maine, for example, has a tendency to swim upside down beneath small boats and surface, bouncing the boat gently on its belly—an activity sure to get a rise out of even the most stout-hearted boater. I've also seen another young humpback in the same area entice people to the edge of a boat rail by swimming within inches of the hull and, just when the unsuspecting whale watchers are hanging over the side scrambling for photos, blow its oily, mucous-filled breath right in their faces, leaving its mark on yet another generation of startled tourists.

The moment that sent my heart pounding with this little calf, though, was when it suddenly clasped my arm between its two pectoral fins and held on for dear life. And life was precisely what I started to think a lot about at that moment. Don't get me wrong. This new approach had its magic, but unlike the manatee, I need to breathe fairly frequently. I could see the headlines; "Man Drowned by Amorous Calf" was one that kept flashing in my mind.

I recalled seeing a photo in *National Geographic* some years before showing a manatee grabbing a researcher's leg in a harmless display of interest. In his book *Ecology and Behavior of the Manatee in Florida*, biologist Daniel Hartman, tells of a similar calf he met in Crystal River who "was extremely forward in her attentions," nuzzling his facemask, nibbling his drysuit, clutching his body with her flippers, and pulling him below the surface. At one point it even embraced his head and tore off his facemask. His research was conducted over twenty years ago, so it was safe to assume this was not the same animal, although it certainly seemed like a close relative.

Despite the calf's size and weight, its grasp was actually quite delicate and obviously not meant to injure me. It was more like a child grabbing on to beg for more play. The difference, of course, was that this was taking place underwater, so with a firm tug I pulled my arm out from between its pectoral fins and backpedaled to regain my balance. By this time a crowd of snorkelers had quickly gathered, and there were suddenly many more people from which to solicit contact. Without so much as a backward glance, my dance partner swam on to choose a new beau.

On my many trips to Florida I've had similar unforgettable visits with manatees who, in addition to the usual physical similarities, have specific traits that set them apart, proving that personality is not something found only in humans. Adjectives like shy, humorous, reclusive, playful, aggressive, curious, even confused are all appropriate when describing manatees, although scientists tend to shudder at this sort of anthropomorphism. And perhaps with good reason. Manatees are manatees, nothing more, nothing less. Their traits and lifestyle are the result of eons of evolution, and they were no doubt acting like manatees long before we finally realized it was easier to get around on two legs instead of four.

I've found, however, that people tend to relate to creatures a little better when viewing and measuring in our own distinctly human way, as egocentric as that may be. Animals that tend to display human-like traits are a lot more popular in the public mind than creatures that don't. For example, it's hard to imagine an alligator getting the same sort of "Isn't he cute?" response as your typical neighborhood dog. We inevitably relate animal behavior to our own reactions to the natural world, assigning to them traits and feelings that are distinctly human. In the same way, a name given by biologists to a whale, manatee, or any creature under study not only helps in identification, but it also imbues an animal with a personality that sets it apart from the crowd. It then becomes something more than a wild animal. It becomes one of us, with thoughts, feelings, and characteristic reactions that make it different and identifiable.

I have had many encounters with manatees that, for one reason or another, make the individuals stand out in my memory. The visits were short so I never took the time to name them, but I can still recall each one by its human personality traits. Take, for example, my meeting with one manatee I simply refer to as the grandmother.

Unlike great whales, which are easy to spot at great distances by their bushy blows or active surface behaviors, manatees rarely cause more than a casual ripple at the surface. For the most part, they move as slowly and deliberately as their ponderous size indicates, occasionally rolling at the surface or poking their snouts out for a snort of air in a quiet, unassuming way.

One blustery February day a few years ago, some friends and I were attempting to snorkel with the manatees in Kings Bay, but the unseasonably warm weather had scattered the population so thoroughly that none were to be found. After exploring the main spring, we decided to head to the north side of Banana Island into a large section of the bay to try our luck.

As our boat drifted slowly into the bay, we strained every sense for any sign of our quarry and were startled by a deep, sharp snort behind us: the characteristic chuffing sound of a manatee breathing at the surface. The exhalation was much louder and more pronounced than usual, sounding almost like a short coughing roar. Turning, we caught a brief glimpse of an extremely large grizzled snout submerging not 25 yards off the port side, its shiny, light-gray skin contrasting sharply with the reflection of the dark blue sky off the water.

Since I was the only one still wearing all my gear, I volunteered to slip into the water and swim in the direction of the animal, which had now completely disappeared beneath the surface. Once there, I would raise my hand to indicate the manatee's location so the others could approach at a distance that wouldn't disturb the creature.

Visibility was poor, maybe 10 to 15 feet at best, and silt hung in the water like frozen pieces of dust drifting across the liquid landscape. After a minute or two of searching, I glanced back at the boat to reorient myself toward the area where the manatee had surfaced. By now I was totally confused and decided to drift, letting the buoyancy of my wetsuit carry me gently at the surface to avoid making any noise. I had no idea where the manatee had gone, or if it had moved at all. I knew I was in the general vicinity but with such limited visibility in 10 feet of water, the best chance for sighting the creature was to wait for it to resurface.

At least seven or more minutes had passed since the animal submerged. I was certain it would surface at any moment, as most resting manatees will take a breath of air every three to five minutes, although they're capable of staying down much longer. This manatee was clearly an exception to the rule.

After drifting for several minutes, I was about to give up and return to the boat, assuming the animal had snuck away, when a fantastically large, boulder-like gray form began to take shape in the greenish mist ahead.

My adrenalin began to pump. This was the largest manatee I had seen before or since. Its incredible size was matched by its girth. I was dwarfed by comparison to its length, which, even allowing for underwater distortion, seemed at least double my size.

Since female manatees tend to grow to greater lengths and weights than males, I assumed I was looking at a grandmother of the species, a wily old behemoth whose experience had taught her to wait out her pursuers. I was certain my approach had gone unnoticed because I had struggled to be as stealthy as possible, but even with the addition of a smooth wetsuit and long jet-fins, snorkelers are nothing more than strangers in a strange land: clumsy hulks more in tune with the terrestrial than the undersea world.

I slowly raised a hand to mark my position for the others as I hovered motionless above the perfectly shaped, unmarked tail of the giant. It was a moment of supreme pleasure, a chance to witness a natural scene unchanged for millenia. Surprisingly, the animal bore no scars, only a thick, powdery coating of the brownish-green algae found on the dorsal surface of many manatees. Mixed with the slate-gray coloring of the wrinkled skin, it added to the appearance of old age.

The corpulent giant stayed in the same posture for several minutes, still and stone-like, perfectly content to nuzzle into the soft bottom mud as grains of silt drifted lazily over the gentle curve of its back. There were no visible signs of breathing; no flexing of the rib cage or bubbles escaping from the sealed nostrils. By now a good eight to nine minutes had passed, an unusually lengthy period for the average manatee, and I was beginning to wonder if this was a planned tactic to elude me. Practically all the manatees I have encountered over the years have surfaced every few minutes, although dives of up to twenty-four minutes in duration have been reported in publications discussing manatee physiology. To accomplish these diving feats, the animal's heart rate slows from the usual resting rate of fifty to sixty beats per minute to as low as thirty beats per minute, allowing them to conserve oxygen and extend their dive time. This particular animal had obviously mastered the technique.

As I held my position, drinking in the fascinating scene in all its ancient, simplistic splendor, the manatee suddenly noticed me. In a slow, deliberate manner, the head turned in a graceful "over-the-shoulder" glance back in my direction. There was a pregnant pause as man and manatee contemplated each other, evaluating choices based on separate experiences. In the gaze of this lone giant there was a certain cleverness, a confidence born of experience, which momentarily bridged the wide gap between wild animal and man.

Although the manatee brain is small, its capabilities must certainly reflect the remarkable adaptive evolution shown by the body's outer core. But this is a question that may never be satisfactorily answered. A debate has raged for years over the relative intelligence of marine mammals, specifically dolphins. But how can we measure the intelligence of other creatures when we have yet to develop an accepted test to measure our own? Intelligence is a difficult concept to define and equally hard to measure. The most logical way to view intelligence may be to measure how well an animal meets its needs relative to its environment. In this case, a manatee lives in perfect harmony with its world, with plenty of food, a long life, no adverse affect on its environment, and no natural enemies save man. In the global perspective, the same cannot be said of the human animal.

Questions of intelligence and environment, however, seemed far too distant and vague as my noble quarry and I exchanged glances. At that moment I found it hard to believe that two such diverse yet similar forms of life could share the same planet for so long in such close proximity and know so little about each other. Be that as it may, an eerie feeling washed over me like the subtle chill from a cool breeze as I realized the game was now reversed—the watched was now doing the watching.

Its gaze was direct and unyielding as if to say, "Okay, you've found me, now what?" There was no playfulness here, no time for games, only deliberate and purposeful action as ancient genetic programming took over. The manatee did what every manatee does when either disinterested or threatened with danger: It left the scene.

Like molten rock, its back rose slowly and gracefully, lifting the great body off the bottom like an airborne dirigible. With a gentle flick or two of its tail the monstrous manatee disappeared into the mist, a surprisingly quick exit for one so large. I was left wallowing in the resulting cloud of silt and mud with only the mental image left to convince me the encounter had been real.

Such memorable visits with wildlife leave lasting impressions that can enhance or even change one's perspectives of the natural world. Manatees, by their inquisitive nature, have left more than the share of lasting impressions, not only on the people who work to save them but also on the general public which can be quick to embrace them if given the opportunity.

In the few short decades since man has nurtured an increased interest in these fascinating mammals, several manatees have achieved a certain celebrity, sometimes deliberate, oftentimes accidental, becoming something more than a face in the crowd.

Over the years occasional stories have surfaced in Florida about individual manatees who have come to rely on human companionship for certain favors. Like the animal that regularly appeared at a marina in Miami to have its belly scratched with a deck brush. Or the large manatee that showed up like clockwork to have the dockmaster at the city yacht pier in St. Augustine scrape barnacles off its back with a paint scraper. These are special creatures who, through their own curiosity and affability, make local headlines as well as new friends. But there are others who have achieved even greater and more lasting fame.

Arguably the most famous of all manatees is one that bore the unusual nickname of Sewer Sam. He rocketed into the public's eye in February 1969 when a construction company working on a Miami project at Northeast 163rd Street and West Dixie Highway called the police to report a 9-foot, 1,200-pound manatee wedged firmly into a 33-inch storm-sewer pipe that ran under the highway. Apparently it had wandered in from one of the many canals in the area and had attempted to swim through the culvert. When police and two state conservation officers were unable to free the animal, they contacted officials at the Miami Seaquarium to request help.

Dr. Jesse White, then the chief veterinarian at the Seaquarium who later achieved some fame of his own for his efforts to breed manatees in captivity, arrived to assess the situation. After placating the frightened animal with bushels of lettuce, Dr. White and his colleagues tied a rope around its body and pulled it free.

The manatee, dubbed Sewer Sam by the local press, was bruised, lacerated, and near death after having been wedged in the storm drain for several days. For the next two years he would undergo rehabilitation in a small 30-foot pool at the Seaquarium, eventually in the company of two other manatees, until officials there decided it was time to release him back to the wild. After thriving in captivity on 100 pounds of the choicest iceberg lettuce each day, however, biologists were concerned that he would not readily readapt to life in the wild, a concern that remains viable with any manatee raised or kept in captivity for an extended period of time.

The answer to Sewer Sam's problems came in the shape of a famous ocean explorer known the world over—Jacques-Yves

Cousteau. In early 1971, Cousteau and his team worked with Seaquarium officials to conceive a release plan for Sam that would be filmed for later use on the renowned television program, "The Undersea World of Jacques Cousteau." In March of that year, Sewer Sam's pool was drained just enough to allow four or five men to maneuver him into a large shipping crate lined with water-soaked foam, which was then hoisted out of the pool and placed onto the back of a flat-bed truck.

Accompanied by Dr. White and Warren Zeiller, curator of fishes at the Seaquarium, Sewer Sam was eventually loaded aboard a C-46 cargo plane for a 600-mile flight north to the tiny town of Brooksville near his final destination, Crystal River. There, in a small enclosed body of water called Three Sisters Springs, he was to be released into a natural environment where he would remain under close observation for a short time behind a temporary man-made barrier to ensure he acclimated properly to the world he had left behind two years before.

At his destination just a couple of hours after leaving the Seaquarium pool, a Cousteau diver upended Sam's shipping crate to introduce the confused traveler to his new home. Reluctantly, Sam edged his way out, first nosing along the edge of the crate then bursting forth with great enthusiasm when the warm fresh waters of the spring filled his sinking crate.

For two weeks he was kept under close observation by Dr. White, the Cousteau team, and Daniel Hartman, who was invited to lend his expertise to the release. During that time, Sam fed voraciously on foods found in the spring, occasionally accepting handouts of water hyacinths that were brought in by Cousteau's divers to encourage him to eat.

Part of the release plan included outfitting the unwary manatee with a small harness encasing a tiny transmitter, which would allow officials to track Sam's progress once he was released into the open waters of Crystal River. Sam, however, was not overly enthusiastic about the idea. Theoretically, the harness, which looked like a vest with two holes for the pectoral fins, was to fit across Sam's midsection, allowing him to swim comfortably, unimpeded by the presence of the transmitter. But putting the vest on Sam was like trying to outfit an elephant with underwear. Much to the chagrin of the divers who attempted to attach the device, they just couldn't get the grudging animal to accept it. So the crew went back to the drawing board and designed a circular harness that fit around Sam's peduncle, where the body tapers down to the start of the tail. The new design, a precursor to the standard design of radio-tracking devices used today, proved much more practical. After a few tries, the transmitter was attached and operating.

Finally, a full two weeks after he was first set free in the spring, the last barrier to Sam's freedom was removed. For the next several days the release team followed his progress by listening for the short pings emitted by the transmitter. At first, Sam was reluctant to leave the spring, dawdling for the first day or so at the outlet as he munched on the water hyacinths that grew in profusion there. Three days later he was sighted in the company of several other manatees, obviously acclimating very well to his new home.

Eventually, contact with Sewer Sam was lost. His story, however, hit television screens around the globe later that year in "The Forgotten Mermaids," one of the first TV specials to focus on the plight of the manatee. Chances are still quite good that one of these days someone will report encountering a particularly friendly manatee sporting a distinctive white spot on the bridge of its snout. Then we'll know for sure that Sewer Sam is doing just fine.

Reintroducing rehabilitated animals back into the wild has become common since Sam's escapade back in the early 1970s. However, releasing manatees who were born in captivity and have never known life in the wild was a great unknown until Sunrise and Savannah, a male and female, respectively, made news in 1986.

Born and bred at the Miami Seaquarium, both manatees were moved in August 1984 to holding pens at Florida's Homosassa Springs Nature World on Florida's west coast to allow them time to adapt to a natural setting while still under the observation of a veterinarian. The idea was simple: Use animals bred in captivity to replace those lost in the wild. Despite the fact that many scientists had already realized that manatees breed too slowly to make this a viable option for preventing the extinction of wild manatees, there were many questions still to be answered about the abilities of captive manatees to survive in the wild.

For the next nineteen months, Sunrise and Savannah adjusted well to their new home in the Homosassa River, eating the endemic aquatic vegetation and adapting well to the river environment. In preparation for their release, radio tracking devices were looped around their tails in the hopes of following their progress over the months to come. On March 28, 1986, the final barrier was lifted, and Sunrise and Savannah swam to freedom under the electronic "eyes" of Dr. Jesse White and his staff, who had overseen the project from the beginning.

After just over two weeks, contact with both animals was lost. Three months later Savannah's tracking device was found by a biologist. It had broken free at a point in the tether that was designed to snap in case the device snagged on something that impeded the manatee's progress. In November, the same equipment from Sunrise was found by a shrimp trawler working the waters 6 miles offshore in the Gulf of Mexico. Although the loss of their radio tags doesn't necessarily mean both animals came to a bad end, neither Sunrise nor Savannah has been sighted since.

Although both animals were healthy and familiar enough with their new local environment, trouble may have begun when they took off for unfamiliar territory. As calves, manatees remain dependent on their mothers for up to two years. Many spend at least their subadult lives within range of the cow. This is most likely a survival technique as it allows the mother to pass along vital information concerning migration routes, feeding grounds, and winter refuges. Two animals raised in captivity like Sunrise and Savannah never had these advantages and could have strayed too far out to sea or gotten lost and disoriented. We may never know. Unfortunately, their release probably generated more questions than it answered.

While Sewer Sam was garnering attention on an international scale and Sunrise and Savannah were making science news, another manatee was living quietly in a small, fresh-water pool at a museum not far from Crystal River. Its fame may not be so widespread, its story not quite so dramatic, but in its own way, the saga of Snooty the Manatee says a lot about survival and the pluck of these creatures and may ultimately teach scientists much about the life expectancy of manatees, at least those raised in captivity.

Snooty's story began on July 1948 in the well-trafficked waters of Biscayne Bay near Miami when a boater failed to see a manatee resting inches from the surface in the waters dead ahead. With a sickening, bone-jarring thud, the craft's propeller sliced deep gashes across the unsuspecting manatee's back, badly mangling the poor creature. As the stunned animal wallowed in shock, officials from the Miami Seaquarium were called in. Without hesitation, they initiated a full-blown rescue effort, containing the injured manatee in a sling, then hoisting their precious cargo onto a truck for the short ride to the aquarium. During the initial examination at the aquarium, the staff veterinarian made a startling discovery. They weren't dealing with just one manatee, they had two to worry about; the bruised, battered, and gashed victim was a pregnant female in the latter stages of pregnancy.

As the days wore on, concern grew that the mother was not capable of coping with the stress of a natural birth. Despite the fact that they had stabilized her, the injuries were too severe and the risk too great. Shortly afterward, on July 21, the mother gave birth by cesarean section to a healthy 60-pound male who was given the nickname Snooty. The little calf, the first manatee born in captivity, was healthy and unfazed by the traumatic injuries that eventually claimed its mother's life just six months later.

In 1949, the little orphan was trucked to Bradenton, a small town in Manatee County on the west coast of Florida, to be the official mascot for the county and to be a part of the DeSoto Celebration, an annual festival. For the next seventeen years he would live a solitary, quiet life in a small, dark tank on Memorial Pier as part of the South Florida Museum, never knowing the companionship of one of his own kind, never experiencing life beyond the four cold walls that entrapped him.

In 1966 things began to look up a bit for Snooty as he took up residence in a new 12-by-20 foot fresh-water pool built just for him at the new location of the South Florida Museum and Bishop Planetarium. Since then he has thrived on four feedings a day, typically consisting of twenty-four heads of lettuce (Romaine is his favorite), sixteen carrots, and six apples—in all, a total of 50 pounds of food costing well over five hundred dollars a month to supply. This healthy diet, which is occasionally supplemented by vitamins, has allowed him to grow to well over 8 feet in length and 700 pounds in weight.

Over 75,000 people a year make the trip to visit Snooty, whose fame continues to grow beyond the county he has called home for well over forty years. He is now the oldest manatee in captivity, a distinction that has brought numerous celebrities as well as scientists to his poolside to visit and study the aging orphan.

According to Jennifer Hamilton, curator of the museum, Snooty has a particular fondness for pineapples, strawberries, and, she adds with evident delight, pretty blond women and ladies with potent perfume. "Usually when we have a large group of visitors, Snooty will swim around the edge of the pool to check out the crowd, pausing especially long where he might smell a familiar or particularly powerful perfume. Often he'll choose someone in the crowd to pick on, hauling himself well up on the edge of the pool with his pectoral fins to nuzzle in a little closer. He's especially adept at remembering faces, even if he hasn't seem them for a long time. He likes people. He genuinely does. I'm certain he thinks he's a person."

Jennifer may be closer to the truth than she realizes, considering that Snooty has met only one of his own kind on one brief occasion. Several years ago an injured calf was brought into the museum pool to spend the night. Jennifer can't recall any particularly unusual reaction on Snooty's part other than an uncharacteristic shyness that kept him from closely investigating the tiny visitor. In the morning, the calf was transferred out and life for Snooty returned to normal.

In any debate about large marine mammals kept in captivity, there are some very good arguments on both sides of the issue. A concrete or fiberglass tank is not a natural home for any animal, and it is indeed sad to think a creature as beguiling as Snooty has never known (nor will ever know) the freedom of his natural habitat. (There is, however, a movement underway to get Snooty moved to a state park so he can be in the presence of other manatees.) On the other hand, his special sort of magic has touched literally millions of people over his lifetime and most likely will continue to do so for years to come. Snooty's annual birthday celebration, for example, has become something of a tradition for generations of Floridians. Mothers who, as children, came to celebrate Snooty's birthday now bring their own children to take part in the free event, which draws over three thousand people each year.

"A lot of our visitors come from all over the world," noted Jennifer. "Many of these people have never even heard of a manatee, much less seen one. It's fascinating to see their faces when they walk up to the pool and see an animal they never even knew existed. Especially one as large as Snooty."

Snooty's role as representative manatee has had a positive role in educating the public about the need to protect an endangered species. He adds life and personality to a creature most Floridians get to see momentarily, if at all. At the same time, the students and scientists who use the museum's facilities to study Snooty's behavior and physiology add to the growing base of knowledge necessary to understanding these unusual and complex marine mammals.

It's hard to believe that after a visit with Snooty boaters wouldn't think twice while passing through manatee waters. Suddenly manatees are something more than pictures on signs or photos in newspapers. They're like Snooty—living, breathing, warmblooded creatures with personalities and traits all their own.

Even though his life began tragically and has been lived in small spaces no bigger than many living rooms, Snooty has led an effective and purposeful existence, reaching far beyond the narrow confines of his tank to help ensure the continued freedom of others of his species. Not bad for a sheltered, flirtatious, and bewhiskered old guy.

The growing attention paid to manatees in the last decade is due in large part to many of these manatees that have made and continue to make headlines, not only in Florida but increasingly around the country. What were once "forgotten mermaids" are now increasingly familiar natural assets, and the public is finally reacting with appreciation and support.

When a baby manatee was born in a canal next to a small restaurant and bar in New Port Richey, Florida, in June 1988, the owners and patrons there adopted the little calf as their own, naming it after the bar and distributing drinks and pictures in celebration of its birth. Little Louie, as the 3-feet-long, 40-pound calf came to be known, caused a minor sensation and received more than a few headlines in the local newspapers. Along with the obvious commercial advantages, the event also demonstrated the growing sense of personal responsibility that many people feel for maintaining the increasingly threatened population of manatees. Years ago, a similar birth probably would have been met with passive indifference, if given any attention at all.

Times have changed. Attitudes are shifting in a positive direction. Much of this is due to the efforts of the many biologists, volunteers, and activists who have made manatees their life's passion. But credit must also be given to those beloved manatees known to the public whose stories add a distinctively modern touch to the already ancient lore of a legendary creature.

THE HUNTERS

PURSUED

In late August 1990, a lone fisherman, motoring up Little Pottsburg Creek in Jacksonville, Florida, was passing under the Atlantic Boulevard Bridge when he made a grisly discovery. Tied to the bridge abutment was the badly mutilated carcass of a large male manatee, its back, sides, and stomach bearing an incredible number of deep wounds. It had been left secured to the bridge in an attempt to hide the carcass from the authorities.

That same day, officers from the Florida Department of Natural Resources (DNR) confirmed the finding from the overpass. When they returned with the recovery equipment shortly afterward, the carcass had disappeared. It was eventually located floating 7 miles upstream from the bridge in the Trout River. The DNR officers suspected that the carcass had been moved to delay its discovery and to make it appear as if the animal had died as the result of a collision with a boat. The necropsy, however, proved that the cause of death had nothing to do with a boat.

Jim Valade, a DNR marine biologist, assisted by the Jacksonville medical examiner, discovered that the animal had been slashed twenty-seven times with a knife. Worse yet, the head bore a deep wound from a gaff, a metal hook used for spearing or holding large fish. It was clear this peaceable animal had met a horrible death at the hands of someone who had killed for no apparent reason. "It was the worse case I have ever seen in over four years of doing necropsies on manatees," said Valade in a published report.

The discovery of the Pottsburg Creek manatee and the particularly cruel method by which the animal was killed proved a brutal reminder that for some the hunting of manatees, whether for food or for sport, is not totally a thing of the past, even though protective laws have been in effect for many years.

Manatees, like all marine mammals, are federally protected under the Marine Mammal Protection Act of 1972 as well as the Endangered Species Act of 1973, which makes it a violation to "harass, harm, pursue, hunt, shoot, wound, kill, capture, or collect endangered species." Florida law, though, reaches deep into the early history of the settlement of the New World in its efforts to protect manatees, showing that in the eighteenth century the English recognized the importance of Florida's "mermaids." British colonial records from May 1764 contain the following entry:

> *At the Council Chamber Whitehall the 21st of May 1764 by the Right Honourable the Lords of the Committee of Council for Plantation Affairs.*

> His Majesty having been pleased by His Order in Council of the 18th of this Instant, to refer unto this Committee, a Representation from the Lords Commissioners for Trade and Plantations, proposing that an Instruction should be given to the Governor of the Province of East Florida to restrain him from granting to any person whatsoever, without His Majestys particular Orders and directions, those parts of the Coast of the said Province frequented by the Animals called the Manati or Sea Cow, where they have their Echouries [estuaries] or Landing Places.

It is not clear whether this edict was designed to establish manatee sanctuaries to protect the animals or to save the animals as a food source for the Crown. Nevertheless, its effect on preserving the manatee population was neglible as hunting continued in many parts of Florida, with both Indians and settlers, some of whom were Spanish or French by descent, capturing manatees for the meat, hide, and ivory-like bones. Visiting the Florida Keys in 1832, John James Audubon described his guide's previous occupation: "For years his employment had been to hunt those singular animals called Sea Cows or Marratees, and he had conquered hundreds of them, 'merely,' as he said, because the flesh and hide bring 'a fair price' at Havannah." Since the guide sold his catch in Cuba, it's quite possible he captured many of his victims outside Florida. Nevertheless, Audubon's comments show that there was a healthy market for the animals, which indicates that demand, and probably hunting activity, was significant.

In 1893 another law protecting manatees was passed in Florida, followed fourteen years later by the establishment of a five-hundred-dollar fine for any person found to have killed or molested one of the mammals. Clandestine killing of manatees continued, though, and reports of manatee poaching were common, especially during the 1930s and 1940s when the hardships of the Great Depression and World War II made meat an increasingly valuable commodity. In the years since, widespread poaching has declined, although scattered reports, similar to the Pottsburg Creek killing, trickle in from time to time. Protection increased significantly in 1978 when the Florida Manatee Sanctuary Act established the entire state as a "refuge and sanctuary for the manatees," allowing for the enforcement of boat speed regulations in designated areas.

In light of their accessibility and desirability as a food source, it is truly a wonder that manatees have even survived to the present day. Their valuable bone, meat, and hide, together with their riverine habitat and nonaggressive manner, have all contributed to their demise over the past several centuries. A strong man armed with a sharp spear and patience was all it took to subdue these plump, slow giants. The arrival of firearms in the New World made the game even easier, and it wasn't long before officials governing colonial Florida realized protection was necessary, hence the the edict of 1764.

Contrary to popular thinking, though, hunting pressures did not reduce the range of the Florida manatee from a more widespread distribution in the southeastern United States. Archeological evidence dating back to about 8500 to 6000 B.C., along with written reports from the colonial era and current knowledge about the physiological traits of manatees prove instead that their range has not changed dramatically. Manatee remains have been found, only in small numbers, at Florida archeological sites but nowhere else in the Southeast. Because manatees are tropical mammals subsisting on a low-energy food base, the northern Gulf of Mexico and the southern part of Georgia represent a climatic barrier above which winter survival is not possible, excepting the few animals that find modern artificial warm-water sources near paper mills and other industries on the Georgia coast.

Understanding the role of manatees in the lives of prehistoric Florida Indian tribes is more difficult because evidence is sketchy. Archeologists generally agree that manatees were not very numerous in pre-Columbian times, although knowledge of the species was widespread among the tribes of the region. Ceremonial smoking pipes in the shape of manatees were widely used, and manatee bones have been found in pre-Columbian middens, the trash heaps of the era, but not in large enough numbers to indicate the animals played anything other than a supplemental role in the everyday diet of the natives. However, the culture and economies of the early Indians, who were much more numerous prior to the arrival of European colonists, were intricately tied to hunting and fishing, so it is safe to assume that they did exert some pressure on the existing manatee populations. The actual numbers of manatees living prior to the discovery of the New World, though, will forever remain a tantalizing mystery.

With the arrival of the Spanish in the sixteenth century, the written record of the exploitation of the manatee in the Americas began in earnest as the Spanish quickly realized the value of such a large, edible animal that could be so easily captured. One of the first Spaniards to describe a manatee, Oviedo y Valdés, writing in 1526, waxed poetic about its beefy taste, describing it as a "fish" with wonderful medicinal properties. He noted that its ear bones—the stapes of the inner ear—which he refers to as "stones," were useful for curing side pains. His description for the preparation of the medicine may say more about the medical practices of the time than it does about the medicinal value of manatee ear bones:

First the stone is burned, then pulverized. When the pain appears, the patient takes his powder in the morning on an empty stomach. He takes as much as can be picked up on a small coin and follows it with a swallow of good white wine. After continuing this treatment for three or four mornings the pain disappears.

It is my guess that the white wine taken in repeated doses over several days did more for treating pain than the bone powder. But the supposed curative powers of the ear bones shows up repeatedly in early literature discussing manatees in the New World, possibly indicating that they were already valued by Indians throughout the Americas before the arrival of the Europeans. Indeed, John R. Swanton, in his book *The Indians of the Southeastern United States*, wrote that "two large bones" taken from the head of the manatee were placed in a chief's grave by the south Florida tribes, a clear indication of their ritualistic importance to the natives.

Eventually the powdered "stones" were touted by the Spanish and English as a remedy for a wide variety of physical ailments, including kidney problems, colic, dysentery, and as "an extraordinary medicine in the stone [colic] or stoppage of water." The Spanish used the powder to alleviate the pain of childbirth, a practice that continues today in Panama. The ear bones are also considered by some Central Americans to be a powerful charm against witchcraft or ill luck and are often worn as pendants.

To reach these conclusions about an animal they knew little about, the Spanish must have relied on the Indians to teach them about both the "medicinal" value of the manatee and the methods used to capture it. Yet, there are no detailed accounts describing manatee hunting by the Indians in the writings of the Spanish colonists. However, one early Spanish writer, Lopez de Velasco, gave a brief description of the method used by the Tekesta Indians of southeast Florida: "When [the hunter] discovers a sea cow he throws his rope around its neck, and as the animal sinks under the water, the Indian drives a stake through one of its nostrils, and no matter how much it may dive, the Indian never loses it, because he goes upon its back."

When I first read this account I thought it was a stretch of the imagination to think that an animal the size of a manatee could be captured in such a manner. Although docile by nature, they are known to thrash and roll violently when caught in nets during rescue operations, a feisty characteristic that could be injurious, even fatal, to the unwary bystander hit by the thrust of a frightened, half-ton animal. Since manatees cannot breathe through the mouth, plugging their nostrils would induce suffocation, although I couldn't imagine one staying still long enough to take such abuse. However, as recently as 1978, this unusual technique was used by *mariscadores*, the subsistence fishermen who live far up along the remote tributaries of the Amazon. To capture the Amazonian manatee, which is smaller than its West Indian cousin and distinctively marked by large pinkish-white marbled blotches on its belly, the *mariscador* hunted at night with a harpoon featuring a detachable head connected by line to a float. After striking the manatee, the hunter clutched the float to his belly, letting the terrified animal pull him and his canoe along. After several dives, the exhausted manatee would surface for an extended time as it struggled to regain its breath. At that point, the *mariscador* paddled up and stuffed the distended nostrils with wooden plugs, inducing suffocation. Quartered and fried in its own fat, the flesh would keep for years in 20-liter kerosene cans.

William Dampier, the famed English buccaneer who wrote four books highlighting his extensive travels throughout the world in the seventeenth century, provides a detailed description of a different type of hunt for manatees he witnessed off the coast of present-day Nicaragua on a visit there in 1681. The hunters were Mosquito Indians, a small Central American tribe that lived along the eastern coasts of Honduras and Nicaragua. The Mosquitos shared with the English a hatred for the Spanish and were often found sailing with English buccaneers, as the stout Indians were highly valued for their hunting and fishing skills. Dampier wrote glowingly of the Mosquitos, noting that they had "extraordinary good Eyes, and discry a Sail at Sea farther, and see any Thing better than we." He goes on to describe their great valor, their remarkable skills with rifles, which they had learned to use while sailing with privateers, and their absolute loyalty to the English.

While sailing south along the Central American coast, Dampier put in to a small bay to careen the ship. While there, his Mosquito men went out in their canoe and captured some manatees. His description may be the most detailed existing depiction of a manatee hunt from that era:

One of the *Moskitoes* (for there go but two in a Canoa) sits in the stern, the other kneels down in the head, and both paddle till they come to the place where they expect their game. Then they lye still, or paddle very softly, looking well about them; and he that is in the head of the Canoa lays down his paddle, and stands up with his striking staff in his hand. This staff is about 8 foot long, almost as big as a mans Arm, at the great end, in which there is a hole to place his Harpoon in. At the other end of his staff there is a piece of light Wood called Bobwood, with a hole in it, through which the small end of the staff comes, and on this piece of Bobwood, there is a line of 10 or 12 fathoms wound neatly about, and the end of the line made fast to it. The other end of the line is made fast to the Harpoon, which is at the great end of the staff, and the *Moskito* man keeps about a fathom of it loose in his hand. When he strikes, the Harpoon presently comes out of the staff, and as the Manatee swims away, the line runs off from the bob; and although at first both staff and bob may be carried under water, yet as the line runs off it will rise again. Then the *Moskito* men paddle with all their might to get hold of the bob again, and spend usually a quarter of an hour before they get it. When the Manatee begins to be tired, it lyeth still, and the *Moskito* men paddle to the bob and take it up, and begin to hale in the line. When the Manatee feels them he swims away again, with the Canoa after him; then he that steers must be nimble to turn the head of the Canoa that way that his consort points, who being in the head of the Canoa, and holding the line, both sees and feels which way the Manatee is swimming. Thus the Canoa is towed with a violent motion, till the Manatee's strength decays. . . . At length when the Creatures strength is spent, they hale it up to the Canoas side, and knock it on the head, and tow it to the nearest shore where they make it fast . . . .

Dampier was amazed by the skill and dexterity of these experienced hunters. "I have known two Moskito men for a week every day bring aboard two Manatee," he marveled, "the least of which hath not weighed less than 600 pound, and that in a very small Canoa, that 3 English men would scarce adventure to go in."

This method of hunting sounds very similar to techniques used by natives of both coasts of North America to hunt whales and porpoises. The Indians of Cape Cod, for example, would frequently venture out into the open Atlantic in fragile canoes to capture the slow swimming right whales that frequented those waters, using numerous harpoons and floats to subdue the 65-foot giants that weighed a ton per foot and which would, fortunately for the hunters, float when dead. As hazardous as it may sound, and it most certainly was, it still seems a lot more efficient than ramming wooden plugs into the snouts of manatees or, in the case of whales, pounding wooden stakes into their blowholes, reputedly a technique used by some coastal tribes in North America. The harpoon and float method was adapted by the white man to capture whales and was common throughout the heyday of the great Yankee whaling era until the onset of the harpoon gun. Looking back, it is remarkable that native American techniques for hunting large marine mammals bore such remarkable similarities despite thousands of miles of distance between their various cultures.

In societies around the world, ritual played an important role in the hunt for any large mammal, often reaffirming a hunter's ties to the natural world while at the same time serving as a demonstration of respect for a noble quarry. Native whale hunters in the American Northwest, for example, often spent days in preparation for hunting the gray whale, taking ritual baths, eating only certain foods, sometimes even mimicking the hunt with other tribesmen to bring luck and to appease the whaling spirits. Although little is known about pre-Columbian rituals concerning manatee hunts, many tribes probably attached some ritualistic significance to an animal that provided such a substantial amount of food and by-products. As recently as the late 1960s, the Rama Indians of Nicaragua took ceremonial baths in manatee blood after the hunt; and the tribesman who harpooned the animal, one of only a few "designated manatee hunters," would return the bones to the area where he killed the animal, believing this would help him find manatees in later forays. The Rama avoided talking about the charms they carried or about the location of the manatees during the hunt as they believed the manatee possesses a keen sense of hearing and will know what is going on. It is quite possible that early explorers observed similar rituals throughout the subtropics and tropics of the New World because manatees were venerated through-out the region when the Europeans first arrived.

The flesh, fat, skin, and bones of manatees were put to an infinite variety of uses limited only by the imagination of the hunter. Its meat was likened to pork or veal in taste and texture and was highly regarded by both the European settlers and the natives. When boiled in its own oil, manatee meat could be preserved for an entire year before going rancid. This unique preservation character-istic enticed one enterprising Dutch company to charter ships in 1643 for the sole purpose of sailing to Guyana to capture manatees, preserve the meat, and transport it to the Caribbean islands, where it was sold as food for slaves. When Sir Walter Raleigh visited Guyana in 1596, he described manatee meat as "wholesome" and "of good flavour," noting that because it came from an animal that lived in the water "Catholics are permitted to use its meat during Lent and other fast days."

Accompanying a voyage of exploration to the Amazon in 1638, Father Cristóbal de Acuña, a Jesuit priest chosen to lead a Spanish clerical delegation to the region, wrote about the wonders of the magnificent river in his book *A New Discovery of the Great River of the Amazons.* He and his colleagues went to great lengths to provide detailed observations to the court of Spain including a review of the outstanding attributes of the Amazonian *pegebuey*, which was his term for what the natives called the *peixe-boi* or manatee. He wrote that "this fish supports itself solely on the herbage on which it browses, as if it were in reality a bullock. . . . And from this circumstance the flesh derives so good a flavor, and is so nutritious, that a small quantity leaves a person better satisfied and more vigorous than if he had eaten double the amount of mutton."

Monsieur Pomet, chief druggist to the French King Louis XIV, extolled the virtues of manatee meat and fat in his book *A Compleat History of Druggs*, published in 1737, noting that "the Flesh tastes like Veal, but it is a great deal finer, and cover'd in several Parts, with three or four Fingers thick of Fat, of which they make *Lard*, as they do of Hog's. This is excellent, and several People melt it and cast it into Cakes, which they eat with Bread instead of Butter." He was less enthusiastic about the salted flesh, which he claimed lost its taste in the drying process and became "as dry as Wood."

Pomet also discussed the value of the head "stones" mentioned earlier, noting that they resembled ivory but were much harder, with wonderful medicinal properties. "It is a fix'd *Alcali*," he says, which "absorbs Acids, eases the Pain of the Stomach, cures Heart-burnings and the Cholick; is good against Stone and Gravel, and to expel Urine." Referring to the value of manatee meat in the Caribbean, he also pointed out that "the Flesh of this Animal makes a considerable Part of the Food of the Inhabitants of those Countries: They carry several Ship-Loads of it every Year from *Terra firma*, and the neighbouring Isles, and as well at *Guadaloupa*, *St. Christophers*, *Martinico*, as other adjacent Islands, they sell a Pound of it for a Pound and a half of Tobacco."

One visitor to the Honduran coast in 1825 wrote that "the flesh of this animal is particularly admired, and thought to resemble very closely that of veal; the tail, which forms the most valuable part of the manati, after laying some days in a pickle prepared for it with spices, etc., and eaten cold, is a discovery of which Apicus might have been proud, and which the discriminating palate of Eloyabalus would have thought justly entitled to the most distinguished reward."

A seventeenth-century traveler also wrote of a particular fondness for the tail: "The tail is cut into pieces and put into the sun for 4 or 5 days, it appears to be nothing but a nerve, but after the moisture is dry'd away, they put it into a pan, and fry it, it turns to butter mostly, which is very proper never turning rancid though kept very long, and being good to fry eggs in, for lamps and medicines."

When Alexander von Humboldt visited South America between 1799 and 1804, he wrote of how the Jesuits there gathered every year to hunt for manatees to obtain a fat, used in their church lamps, that "has not the fetid smell of whale-oil." These same men would cut the hide into strips which served "like thongs or ox-leather, to supply the place of cordage."

Dried strips of manatee hide must have been remarkably resilient, as they were used for making a variety of items for which leather was the usual material, including shoes, horse whips and whips that were shipped to Caribbean plantations to be used on slaves. Dampier noted that manatee skin was also "of great use to Privateers, for they cut them out into straps, which they make fast on the sides of their Canoes, through which they put their Oars in rowing, instead of tholes or pegs." The ancient Maya also reportedly used manatee hide on their canoes—not for oar locks, but as a durable sheath in the same manner North American Indians used birch bark to cover their canoes. Some South American Indians even used shields and wore foot coverings made from the material.

Although the true extent to which manatees were exploited in the Americas before the arrival of Europeans will never be known, it is clear they were being hunted by natives throughout their subtropical and tropical range in the early 1500s. Before then, all is a mystery. However, in his paper, *The Pre-Columbian Exploitation of the Manatee in Mesoamerica*, anthropologist Dr. Richard Bradley theorizes that the manatee may have played a vital role in the cultural development of the mysterious Olmec civilization, which flourished for eight centuries in the hot, humid plain of the Veracruz gulf coast starting around 1200 B.C. Before their sudden and inexplicable disappearance, the Olmec left testimonials to prodigious human labor, including massive sculptures, cave paintings, and boulder reliefs in what many scholars believe is Mesoamerica's first great art style. Their legacy would endure to become part of other great cultures, including that of the Classic Maya. According to Bradley it is possible, though not widely accepted, that the art of the Olmec may also reflect a strong cultural tie to manatees. Many of their carvings of deities have distinctive features such as flippers; thick, almost nonexistent necks; cleft lips; and truncate muzzles, bearing a striking resemblance to manatees. One of their gods is even depicted with vegetation springing from its body in what may be a clear representation of a feeding manatee.

Most anthropologists, however, believe that the Olmec primarily exploited other aquatic species such as fish and turtles, and indeed there is little mention of manatees in the discussions of Olmec subsistence. But Dr. Bradley argues that this is a result of a general lack of familiarity with the mammals on the part of anthropologists and a lack of "a systematically compiled data base." He alone believes that the manatee may have been an important food source and a religious symbol for the Olmec and may have flourished in the waters near three key Olmec sites—San Lorenzo, Tenochtitlán, and Potrero Nuevo—which "were interconnected politically, culturally, and socially in ancient times." Because manatees were a year-round resource that would have provided tremendous amounts of protein, Dr. Bradley theorizes that an elite group may have risen among the Olmec who controlled river levee areas where manatees congregated and, as a result, held considerable power over communities dependent upon a reliable protein supply. In their attempt to maintain economic control over the outlying populace by providing a much needed steady food supply, the Olmec elite may have overexploited the manatee. As a result, Bradley theorizes, they may have resorted to building artificial lagoons in which to breed and raise manatees. Over twenty of these lagoons, some of which are lined by bentonite blocks and fed by elaborate aqueduct systems, have been found intact at San Lorenzo.

As intriguing and plausible as Dr. Bradley's theories may be, there is little evidence to confirm them. Perhaps at some point in the future more artifacts will surface to provide an undeniable link between the manatee and the rise of an advanced civilization now lost deep in the shadows of the distant past.

If indeed the Olmec raised manatees in artificial lagoons, they may have been the first to exploit manatees under controlled conditions—but not the last. Since manatees and dugongs are the only known mammals able to convert aquatic vegetation into protein, there has been some discussion over the years focused on raising them commercially, like beef cattle. In 1893, a group of entrepreneurs wanted to turn 100,000 acres of water in Manatee Bay, south of Miami, into a manatee farm to raise the animals for their meat, bones, and hide. It never went further than the planning stages. Then again, in 1917, Alexander Graham Bell, the man to whom we owe so much of our present communication capabilities and a master inventor who never lacked for entrepreneurial ideas, proposed the idea of a manatee farm. Although this too went nowhere, it did catch the notice of William Beal, a veterinary officer in West Africa, who explored the idea of raising West African manatees in lagoons. Like the others, he probably discovered that the slow reproduction rate of the animals, the lack of knowledge about manatees, and the technology of the time made the idea impractical.

There is one characteristic of manatees that has been used successfully to benefit mankind directly—their voracious appetite. In the early 1970s, the small South American republic of Guyana asked the National Academy of Sciences in Washington, DC, to develop solutions to the growing problems caused by the proliferation of aquatic weeds. At the time, the explosive growth of aquatic weeds was threatening to become one of the world's most significant environmental problems. Irrigation projects were being choked to a slow trickle, shipping was blocked in many small waterways, farmers in Bangladesh faced starvation when rafts of floating weeds smothered the rice crop, and bridges in many Third World countries were bursting from pressure caused by choked off waterways. Areas of the Congo River were so clogged that portions of nearby Zaire had to be abandoned for lack of transport. The weeds were also affecting water quality. One Canadian scientist noted that "an acre of growing water hyacinth imposes an oxygen-depleting load on the water equivalent to the sewage from 40 people." Worse yet, water weeds were a perfect breeding ground for mosquitoes, the dreaded carriers of malaria and encephalitis, the scourge of the tropics. And if all this wasn't bad enough, aquatic weeds encourage the growth of a variety of water-borne illnesses including the world's most prevalent parasitic disease—schistosomiasis.

Among the suggestions provided to Guyana by a meeting of science organizations in 1973 was the utilization of manatees to attack the weeds. The idea was not new. Earlier in this century sugarcane plantation owners in Guyana used manatees to keep irrigation canals clear. From 1959 through the next three years, eighty manatees were also used by Guyana to keep the growth of weeds in check in waterways through the country. A male and female were introduced into a clogged canal that had consistently stymied engineers. Years later the male and female had produced a calf, and all three were so efficient at keeping the canal clear that rangers seldom even took the time to check on them. The reason is simple. The average adult manatee consumes about 10 pounds of food for every hundred pounds of weight. So, if a manatee weighs 1,500 pounds, it will need to consume an amazing 150 pounds of vegetation each day to keep up its ample figure. If all this munching can be concentrated in a single area, the clearing results are nothing short of spectacular. In 1959 town officials in Georgetown, Guyana's capital city, began using two manatees to keep back the weeds in the waterworks' 2,000-foot-long canal, which usually filled solidly with weeds in less than two months. Decades later the manatees were still keeping the canal clear and the weeds trimmed grass-neat at no cost.

The trouble is, manatees are limited to the true tropics or, in the case of Florida, warm water effluents when the weather cools. A mid-1960s experimental canal-clearing project in that state, involving eight manatees, failed when several of the animals died of pneumonia from the cold. Besides the temperature tolerance issue, large river systems would also require substantial herds of the animals to keep up with the growth. Given all the environmental stresses manatees face and their slow rate of reproduction, large herds are simply not feasible. As a result, their use as weed-clearers is limited.

On the other side of the world, in the home of the dugong, there are few options for utilizing these mammals beyond the mainte-nance of native cultures through subsistence hunting. Although protected in most of its range, the dugong is still hunted by some native cultures in the Indo-Pacific region. One of the foremost of these tropical marine hunting societies can be found in the Torres

Strait, between Australia and New Guinea. This area is known as Australia's "marine outback" and is thinly populated and largely undeveloped. The islanders who live on reserves there are allowed to hunt dugongs under a special set of Queensland state laws designed to assist the natives in maintaining traditional cultural ties. And for centuries, tradition has meant dugong hunting.

Most other tropical marine hunting societies have vanished in a flood of change brought about by the introduction of missionaries, cash markets, and environmental awareness. Yet, the Torres Strait islanders have managed to maintain a hold on their traditional ways by adapting outside influences to fit their lifestyle and by using a unique set of rights, granted by Queensland state legislation, which allows them to pick and choose who gets to visit their reserves. While the Queensland government controls most of the finances, transportation, and communication systems for the reserves, the islanders control access, thereby protecting a culture based on kinship and social obligations. Two researchers, Bernard and Judith Nietschmann, were granted access to the islands in 1976 and later published a fascinating report on the islanders for whom hunting is not just a necessity but a "way of life."

In the waters surrounding these granite and coral islands, dugongs thrive on extensive beds of sea grasses and algae. The animals are hunted year-round, but the most favorable conditions occur from December through April, when northwest storms pummel the reefs, prompting the animals to seek the calmer waters in the lee of the islands.

To be a hunter in this area of fluctuating tides, swift currents, fickle winds, and changing water visibility requires a complex and detailed knowledge of the marine environment but also of dugong behavior that is passed from generation to generation. The islanders have over eighty terms for different tides and water conditions and twenty-seven terms to distinguish the sizes, ages, sexes, colors, social groupings, even the taste qualities of dugongs. Experienced hunters can tell the size and sex of a dugong even in turbid water conditions simply by observing its wake and position in a herd. More incredibly, when hunting at night, they are able to distinguish an animal's age and sex simply by listening to its exhalation sounds. They have developed these remarkable skills in response to a challenging hunting environment and long-standing village preferences for the meat and fat from an *ipika dangal* (a female adult dugong), especially a pregnant one. Islanders are very fussy about the quality of the meat and fat and will reject a *wati dangal* (a bad dugong) if the fat is too thin. Since a hunter must be very careful as to the type of dugong he captures, risking shame if his catch is not of acceptable quality, he must be fully aware of all the subtle nuances that provide clues to capturing the best animal possible.

The lead hunter, a *buai garka* (male family head), is greatly respected in the community. He acquires his skills by assisting in hunts starting as a teenager when he is taught to handle and throw a 14-foot harpoon from one of his mother's brothers, called an *audi*, who plays a critical role in the training process. The *audi* acts as a mentor and friend, commanding the utmost respect, and traditionally he is the recipient of the boy's first dugong.

Even after all the skills have been mastered, luck plays a significant role in the success of the hunt. A *buai garka* is careful to ensure that he never wastes meat, is generous with other villagers when distributing his catch, and never takes along a crewman whose wife is pregnant, as all these things can bring bad luck. Good luck, however, can be assured by visiting the graveyard to appeal to the ancestors, being generous to your *audi*, and even by sprinkling generous amounts of salt on the harpoon line. In addition to these generally accepted rules, each hunter has his own time-proven techniques to ensure success, some of which are personal secrets not readily shared.

Hunters will depart only if the tidal conditions are right. Since most hunting takes place in water 12 feet or less in depth, the 11-foot tidal range can swiftly open or close large hunting areas. The availability of dugongs and other marine creatures is intricately tied to the movement of the tides, with the hunt often taking place in the turbid waters in which dugongs prefer to feed. When underwater visibility is poor, or during a night chase, hunters watch for signs that a dugong is near: clouds of whitish silt caused by the uprooting of the grasses on which dugongs feed, floating sea grass, trails of bubbles, or smooth or swirling wakes resulting from underwater movement. After sighting an acceptable target (hunters will not pursue a dugong that is too small to feed many or too large to fit in the boat after capture), the crew maneuvers quietly within harpoon range, a task that requires an accurate estimation of boat drift, the dugong's pattern of surfacing movements, and the edibility of the meat.

Distribution of the meat is a social event shared by the entire village. Once a dugong has been landed, carefully prescribed lines, which haven't changed since ethnographers first reported them in the last century, are carved into the hide to act as cutting guides during the butchering process. The islanders have at least forty-five names for the different cuts of meat. Everyone will receive a portion of the kill if there is enough. If not, the harpooner and his *audi*, oftentimes with the help of village elders, decide who receives a share. First choice goes to the hunter, his boat crew, the *audi*, and his brothers, if he has any; the rest is divided equally among the villagers. Any waste is fed to the sharks as an offering in recognition that they too share the bounty of the sea.

For the Torres Strait islanders, the modern conveniences of aluminum boats, outboard motors, and gasoline have enhanced, but not inherently changed, a traditional way of life. They now buy many household food items from commercial stores, but fresh dugong meat remains a highly desired traditional food which is readily shared among all without the exchange of cash or anything of monetary value. By capturing dugongs and following the ways of their ancestors, these islanders are able to maintain the social values that form the "glue" of their society, retaining a specific identity in a world where most societies have long since become dependent on developed, commercial economies. At the same time, the Nietschmanns report that the dugong population in the region is still high, mostly due to protective legislation, seasonal movements to reefs too distant for the hunters to reach, and reduced hunting pressure resulting from a population shift when many islanders moved to the mainland after World War II.

The issue of subsistence hunting by native cultures is complex and controversial. On the one hand, dugong populations worldwide are threatened, in some areas worse than others, and there's no doubt that every effort should be made to ensure their survival. On the other hand, as technology creates an increasingly homogeneous world, many native cultures are losing their identities; entire societies are left with few traditions to call their own. For many of these people, all that remains of a once proud and dignified lifestyle is hunting, a formalized event that allows them to celebrate and share as a community. But what happens when the animals they hunt are highly endangered species like manatees, dugongs, or—in the case of the Alaskan Eskimos, Indians, and Aleuts—the bowhead whale? Should the hunt continue?

The Bardi tribesmen of northwestern Australia, for example, make a strong case for the importance of dugong hunting in maintaining a tribal identity. Like many Australian aborigines, the Bardi fell victim to the avarice of the white settlers during the settlement of that great land in the 1800s, losing family members to enslavement, lands to development, and dignity to alcohol as they adopted some of the less admirable traits of the white settlers. They finally ended up scattered throughout some of the worst slums of

Derby. Then, only a few short decades ago, two of the tribal elders who remembered better days persuaded the tribe to return to its ancestral lands to reclaim the dignified lifestyle abandoned so long ago. The Bardi are now a thriving, self-sufficient tribe that lives in modern homes, goes to school, and lives off the bounty of the sea, including the substantial dugong population that inhabit the waters off that coast. For these people, as with the Torres Strait islanders, there is a great amount of folklore and cultural significance tied to the hunting of dugongs. Only certain men are allowed to hunt; the others cannot even touch the equipment. They will not undertake a hunt while mourning the death of a relative or after a serious argument, for to do so would not only threaten the availability of dugongs but could also bring disaster and illness upon the tribe. These stringent beliefs, while appearing to be simple superstitions, are actually clever control mechanisms designed to limit the number of potential hunters in the population. For the Bardi, capturing a dugong is the ultimate expression of bravery and achievement and, even though modern equipment like dinghies and outboard motors have replaced traditional hunting gear, tribal mores ensure that there is no indiscriminate hunting or waste. As long as the dugongs survive, so too will the Bardi.

As might be expected, today there is great pressure on the aborigines and the islanders to abandon their traditional ways and fully adopt a "modern" lifestyle, with the attendant problems that have threatened the very existence of their cultures. Alcoholism, the loss of old skills and languages, and the feeling of helplessness that comes with domination by what is essentially a foreign government have put many native Australian cultures at risk. To survive, they maintain a tenuous hold on traditions, such as dugong hunting, which give them self-respect and an independence from government handouts or the goods available for purchase at the village store. To them, the Western idea of conservation is a difficult concept to grasp although, in many ways, through established mores, they have practiced it for hundreds, perhaps thousands, of years.

The argument to ban subsistence hunting says that dugongs and manatees are endangered so all hunting must stop. But, as with all complicated issues, lying beneath the surface are many other factors that must be taken into consideration. Is subsistence hunting one of the main causes of the depletion of dugong or manatee populations? Is the maintenance of cultural traditions integral to the survival of some native populations? How endangered are marine mammals in the regions where hunting is allowed? Do native rights supercede the rights of the animals to survive?

But it's important to note that subsistence hunters are not the only perceived threat to dugong populations. The wide Indo-Pacific distribution of the dugong has made them a target for thousands of years. Today they are still hunted over a large portion of their range, primarily for fresh meat, which tastes like veal or pork. Many of their by-products, like those from the manatee, are considered by numerous cultures to possess wondrous medicinal powers that make them highly prized and valuable. Fishermen in the Aru Islands sell "dugong tears" as an aphrodisiac, carve the bones like ivory, and make cigarette holders out of the short tusks. Today, people in Palau wear the atlas vertebrae as wristlets, a practice first observed in the eighteenth century. The ancient Chinese also believed that many items from dugongs had aphrodisiac properties; they also prized the head "stones" (most likely the tympanic ear bones), believing they could clear obstructions of the kidneys and the digestive system. This medicinal use of powdered ear bones from dugongs slowly made its way from China via merchants, mercenaries, and explorers to the New World and into the medical texts of the English and Spanish, who simply substituted manatee ear bones as the main ingredient. This is an example of how folklore weaves its way through cultures as each race of people assimilates beliefs into its own lore. The folklore of the mermaid most likely traveled a similar path as it grew from a simple tale told in the dark confines of some ancient fo'c'sle to a widespread belief featuring alluring enchantresses of the deep. But for many, it is the dogged belief in the efficacy of the medicinal properties of dugong by-products that has survived the centuries.

Fishermen in Ceylon still use dugong oil as an obstetric remedy as well as for cooking. Inhabitants of the Comoro Islands use dugong bone meal to treat boils. In Madagascar the bone meal is used to treat pulmonary diseases while fat from the head helps soothe headaches and earaches. The body fat, when mixed with rice, is put to a slightly different use as a cathartic and to help treat leprosy and a wide range of skin diseases. In Madagascar, as in many other areas, the butchering of dugongs is a ritualistic affair and is usually completed in total silence with cloths covering the carcass to prevent others from viewing the dead animal. Afterward, the skin is dried for leather and, like the hide of the manatee, is used to make a variety of items, including sandals. One researcher even claims that the ark of the covenant treasured by the ancient Israelites was covered with untanned dugong leather. Because of this, he named the Red Sea dugong *Halicore tabernaculi*.

Despite the vast distances that separate the four living species of *Sirenia*, their histories have paralleled each other in many ways. Even today their problems are all very similar—threatened habitat, continued hunting, and diminished breeding populations. As a result, research biologists working with the various species of *Sirenia* file increasingly dismal reports highlighting the devastation that hunting alone has caused. And it isn't difficult to sense the direction in which all this is going. Along Brazil's north and northeastern coast, the World Wildlife Fund estimates that a mere two-hundred West Indian manatees survive. Their cousins in the Amazon River fare slightly better only because of the vastness of the river and protection under the law, although illegal poaching continues. As long ago as 1978, the *mariscadors* complained that their catch of Amazonian manatees had diminished greatly, from five a night to one a week. This isn't hard to understand in light of the fact that between 1935 and 1954, when manatee hides were in great demand, an estimated two-hundred thousand manatees were harvested from the Amazon. It's horrifying to think of what has happened to the populations of Amazonian manatees in the ensuing years. In Haiti, few fishermen under the age of fifty are able to describe firsthand encounters with manatees simply because so few are ever seen or captured now. The World Wildlife Fund also reports that, despite protection, the manatee in Cameroon, West Africa, which is referred to by some tribes as *mammywater*, has come under increasing pressure from the neighboring Nigerians who illegally hunt the animals and sell the meat back to the Cameroonians. Dugongs have also been all but exterminated from coastal regions of eastern Africa and Asia and face an uncertain future in many other parts of their vast range.

Part of the difficulty in assessing the full damage done to sirenian populations around the world is the remoteness of the regions where they exist, political instability, and a lack of financial support. The extended observations necessary to make clear judgments on what must be done are expensive undertakings operating in sometimes hostile, even dangerous political climates. It would have been more than a bit challenging, for example, to have been studying the dugong populations off Bahrain in the Persian Gulf when war broke out in January 1991. It's equally challenging to sell conservation in a country like Haiti, where poverty and the latest coup make starvation a daily curse and any creature that represents food, like the manatee, a blessing.

It's clear that manatees and dugongs mean different things to different cultures. Those who have the pleasure of living comfortably look at these intriguing marine mammals and see magical and alluring creatures every bit as fascinating as the legends that have sprung up about them; to them the idea of hunting is abhorrent and unnecessary. Others see these mammals as a means of cultural, even physical, survival. The maintenance of ancient traditions or the ability to provide sustenance takes precedence over concerns about the environment and the irreparable ecological damage that may result from long-traditional practices. Conservation may be as foreign a concept to them as luxury. If continued hunting of manatees and dugongs was an issue strictly confined to developed and wealthy countries like the United States, the answers would be clearly on the side of conservation. However, the possible extinction of these endangered marine mammals is a worldwide issue crossing several continents and an infinite number of cultures, all of which face different challenges. The only clear conclusion offered by a review of historical and contemporary facts and issues concerning the order of *Sirenia* is that together these mammals represent a unique rung up the ladder of evolution—a ladder whose space is slowly being reserved exclusively for the rise of man.

A LEGEND LOST: THE STORY OF THE STELLER'S SEA COW

As long as things escape us and perish unknown with our consent, and through our silence are counted as fabulous . . . it is not strange that these things . . . have remained to the present time unknown and unexplored.
—Georg Wilhelm Steller, 1751

It seemed a strange place to come in search of a marine mammal from a distant sea, but the Harvard University Museum of Comparative Zoology in Cambridge, Massachusetts, is one of the few places in the world where I could view a skeleton of one of the earth's most curious, albeit extinct, marine mammals—the Steller's sea cow.

This giant relative of manatees and dugongs lived only around the Commander Islands—Bering and Copper—in the remote reaches of the Bering Sea. Its discovery in 1741 was a godsend to the destitute Russian explorers who were shipwrecked on those cold, lonely islands in November of that year. The survivors, who were at first fascinated by the large herds of these lumbering giants, eventually resorted to butchering the beasts to avoid starvation. Tragically, a mere twenty-seven years after its discovery, the Great Northern sea cow (*Hydrodamalis gigas*) became extinct, vanishing from the face of the earth and the eyes of science, the result of overzealous hunting and callous indifference. Consequently, what is known about this remarkable creature comes from the observations and writings of Georg Wilhelm Steller—a German naturalist and surgeon who was a member of the shipwrecked expedition team—and from scattered reports submitted by Russian fur hunters, mining engineers, and merchants who later came to exploit the resources of the islands.

To say the Harvard specimen of *Hydrodamalis gigas* is rare is a gross understatement. In the museums of the world, there are only ten skeletons of the animal, all of which have been constructed with parts from more than one individual. Two other composite skeletons were destroyed in the bombing of Hamburg and Dresden during World War II. No complete skeleton of a single individual has ever been found.

With this in mind, I ascended the granite steps fronting the imposing red brick building, expecting a dramatic display of the bones featuring large placards proclaiming the specimen's rarity. Instead, the skeleton hangs in a quiet end of the Mammals of the World Hall, directly below the whale bones and surrounded by glass cases full of bleached bones labeled with tongue-twisting names like *Pholidota*, *Tubulidentata*, *Proboscidea*, and *Carnivora*. The last remnants of Stellar's sea cow rest in relative obscurity, ignored by the scores of schoolchildren whose voices echo throughout the vast museum complex. A modest placard in the huge chest cavity notes that the components of this "exceedingly rare" skeleton were collected on Bering Island in 1882 by Dr. Leonard Stejneger, a member of an expedition from the Smithsonian Institution.

Although the bones are large—about 18 to 20 feet from snout to tail by my rough measurement—in comparison to the sperm, finback, and right whale bones that adorn the ceiling above, the sea cow bones look rather modest. Yet for someone trying to visualize the form and shape of a creature extinct for well over two hundred years, they are an invaluable reference, a frame, if you will, upon which to stretch the fabric of imagination. The head is comically small in comparison to the rest of the body. The skull, shaped somewhat like that of a horse, is dwarfed by the amazingly thick bones of the torso and by the cavernous opening formed by the ribs, which taper down to a fine point at the tip of the tail. Two tiny appendages, the flippers, stick out like an afterthought from each side. This was a creature unlike any I had ever viewed, although at first glance, the skeletal form bore a great resemblance to that of manatees and dugongs.

On the diminutive skull is a tiny reference number: 59412. I jotted it down and took it to the museum's information desk to inquire if anyone could tell me something about the origin of the Harvard specimen.

After ascending the ancient steps to the Department of Mammalogy on the fifth floor, I opened the door to the distinctive smell of mothballs. Bones of every size and description are visible behind the glass fronts of row upon row of antique wooden cases all illuminated by buzzing fluorescent lights. Pointing down a long, dimly lit hall a handwritten sign asks visitors to check in at the office.

Wooden floorboards creaked underfoot as I wandered down the musty old corridor. Just past a wall decorated haphazardly with a variety of cattle skulls, the office door stood open. I handed a young co-ed the reference number, and she began searching through several dusty, leatherbound journals full of entries scribbled in longhand. Moments later, she fingered a lone entry on specimen 59412, entered in delicate nineteenth-century script: 1882, Steller's sea cow, "no data available."

I left disappointed, pondering the finality of extinction. Here I was in one of the world's finest museums, custodian of one of the few existing Steller's sea cow skeletons, yet the lone data entry signaled the fractured knowledge, the elements of mystery that will forever encompass the existence of Steller's sea cow. Man's exposure to this unusual beast had been for a brief period of twenty-seven years, with only a single naturalist to describe its appearance and habits. Later I found a clue to the origin of the Harvard skeleton in a

Smithsonian magazine article written by Victor B. Scheffer, noted author and biologist. Scheffer tells of meeting Dr. Stejneger at the Smithsonian in 1941. Stejneger was by then well known as Steller's biographer. When Scheffer met the ninety-year-old Stejneger that day in the National Museum of Natural History, the elderly scholar told of hijacking various sea cow bones from Russian workmen who had excavated them from the sands of Bering Island with the intent of shipping the specimens to St. Petersburg, which was then the Russian capital. By adroitly assigning certain exchanges of gold, Stejneger was able to get the bones shipped instead to the Smithsonian Institution in Washington, DC. Although Scheffer notes that the official reports do not mention the deal for the bones, he guessed the transaction occurred around 1882 or 1883. It's safe to assume, then, that the skeleton that hangs in the Harvard museum may very well be one of the sets of bones Stejneger purchased with gold over a century ago.

The story of the creature and its discovery is as intriguing as its bones are rare. And as it is with so many great discoveries, it happened by accident. In November 1741, the Russian brig *St. Peter*, under the command of Captain-Commander Vitus Jonassen Bering, was returning from an epic voyage of discovery to the northwest coast of America when it was wrecked on one of the remote, uninhabited islands in the far western reaches of the Bering Sea. While reconnoitering the island days after the wreck, Steller, who was acting as physician and mineralogist on the voyage, caught his first glimpse of the giant sea cow while he and an assistant pursued a sea otter: "I saw at the same time on the beach many manatees, which I had never seen before," he wrote in his journal, "nor could I even know what kind of an animal it was since half of it was constantly under water."

Throughout the grueling winter on the barren island, Steller watched the sea cows feeding on the brown and red algae, drifting in and out with the tide, oftentimes so close that he could reach out and stroke their backs from the beach. The giant creatures made tempting targets, but, initially, their great size deterred the fatigued, scurvy-ridden men from attempting to kill them. The harsh and bitter winter wore on. Hunting parties left on daily forays in search of meat, but incessant hunting soon killed off the game nearest camp, necessitating increasingly longer treks of up to 30 miles over the mountains—a journey made even more miserable by tattered, inadequate clothing, and lack of nourishing food.

Shortly after the shipwreck, the crew had begun to build a new vessel, but as the food stores disappeared the carpenters grew weak, complaining that they could never meet their August deadline unless they had something more to eat. At that point the men made up their minds to attempt to capture one of the sea cows. But they were soon to discover that their quarry was every bit as formidable as its size indicated.

On May 21, they manufactured a large iron hook, fastened it to a stout rope, and, while standing at the edge of the shore, attempted to jab the crudely manufactured weapon into one of the giants and pull it ashore. Their first attempt ended in failure as they couldn't puncture the animal's bark-like skin. They solved that problem by changing the angle of the hook, but another quickly surfaced. Once the hook was firmly imbedded, the startled sea cow bolted for the open ocean, escaping with all the equipment and leaving the exhausted hunters with nothing but raw hands to show for the ordeal.

As the men weakened and the situation became more desperate, they decided to repair the ship's wrecked yawl and hunt the creatures utilizing classic whaling techniques. By the end of June 1742, the boat was ready. Immediately six of the strongest men departed for the hunt, five to row and one to act as a harpooner. A long rope, which trailed from the end of the harpoon, was wound neatly in coils in the bottom of the boat, then run all the way to the shore where it was held firmly by forty of the healthiest men.

The hunters rowed quietly toward their prey as the sea cows continued to feed voraciously on kelp, totally unaware of the beginning of a hunt that would soon drive them to extinction. With a powerful thrust, the harpooner struck one of the ungainly beasts, burying the weapon deep into the animal's hide. With all the strength the enfeebled men ashore could muster, they pulled the struggling animal toward the beach while the men in the boat stabbed it repeatedly with large knives and bayonets until, weakened by the large quantities of blood that gushed "like a fountain" from its wounds, the sea cow was pulled ashore at high tide and secured.

As the tide receded, the hapless sea cow was stranded on the exposed beach. The men descended on their catch like wild animals, cutting off large pieces of meat and fat and carting off the spoils to be eaten, stored in barrels, and hung up to dry on racks. "At long last," wrote Steller, "we found ourselves suddenly spared all trouble about food and capable of continuing the construction of a new ship by doubling the workers."

Once he had one of the animals ashore, Steller immediately recognized the scientific significance of the battered hulk that lay on the beach before him. Despite its huge size, it bore a remarkable resemblance to the manatees seen by Spaniards in America, although its horizontal, forked tail was more like a whale's flukes than a manatee's spatulate, spoon-shaped tail.

The starving, emaciated crew had found a true larder in these bizarre creatures. One animal supplied the entire camp with meat for up to two weeks. Steller found the meat indistinguishable from beef, plus it had the unique characteristic of staying edible for over two weeks even during the hottest summer months. He attributed this to the animal's herbivorous and salty diet, which also gave the meat a redder color than that of carnivorous animals. By preserving the muscles of the abdomen, back, and sides in salt, the meat was "in every respect equal to corned beef and most delicious."

The fat, which was "four fingers thick" around the body, was "not oily or flabby but rather hard and glandular, snow-white, and, when it has been lying several days in the sun, as pleasantly yellow as the best Dutch butter." The boiled fat was sweeter and better tasting than beef fat and like olive oil in color and texture. Steller likened the taste to sweet almond oil with "exceptionally good smell and nourishment." He and the other men drank cupfuls of the oil without the slightest bit of nausea, discovering at the same time that it acted as a gentle laxative and diuretic.

With the troublesome task of securing food for the encampment all but eliminated, the men could focus their efforts on completing the ship while Steller turned his full attention to studying the remarkable sea cows. To this day, his detailed descriptions of the animal's appearance, diet, and behavior, made during the remaining months of his confinement on Bering Island, remain the only scientific observations of the living animal. And they form a fascinating portrait of a most unusual creature.

Sea cows lived in vast herds of males, females, and offspring feeding incessantly throughout the year on the algae growing along the coast of Bering and Copper islands. According to Steller, they were "busy with nothing but their food," scraping the kelp off the rocks using hooked forelimbs, the ends of which looked something like a horse's hoof, terminating underneath in a mass of short, densely set bristles similar to a "scrub brush." Steller noted that while feeding, "they move first one foot then the other, as cattle and sheep do when they graze, and thus with a gentle motion half swim and half walk." These forelimbs, which were positioned in the same pectoral area as those of a manatee, were apparently quite different from the paddle-like flippers of both the manatee and dugong.

Steller was so puzzled by the appearance of these appendages that he admittedly didn't know whether to refer to them as hands or feet.

While eating, the sea cows chewed constantly, moving their heads and necks like oxen, and lifting their heads every few minutes to draw a breath that sounded as if they were "clearing their throats like horses." They would feed like this for hours on end, sluggishly moving out and in with the tide, effortlessly maintaining their steering ability in the rough water.

Calves were apparently born throughout the year, although Steller noted seeing more calves in August than at any other time. Since mating took place during June, Steller concluded that the fetus remained in utero for over a year, indicating a slow reproductive rate, a fact which undoubtedly contributed to their rapid demise.

It is easy to understand why they were referred to as sea cows. Besides the obvious physical resemblance to manatees, a familiar creature even in Steller's time, their nonstop grazing and sluggish mannerisms seemed very much like those of the land animals found in barnyards around the world. Even more surprising, they gave milk. Located beneath the forelimbs were two breasts, which terminated in black, wrinkled, 2-inch-long teats blessed with innumerable milk ducts exuding a rich, tasty milk, which, the explorers noted, surpassed the milk of land animals in taste, fat content, and sweetness.

The head of the animal resembled that of a buffalo, especially concerning the straight lips, but was somewhat small in proportion to the rest of the body as evidenced by the Harvard skeleton. The sea cow had no teeth. Instead, Steller found two broad bones, or masticating pads, which were similar to those found in manatees and dugongs, allowing the animals to feed on the soft, nonfibrous kelp that flourished near or at the surface in shallow water. Their feeding style reminded the naturalist of the manner in which a cow crops grass in a field.

Around the lips were numerous bristles, like those found on the snout of a manatee. Steller noted that the bristles were so thick on the lower jaw they resembled "the feather quills of chickens." The eyes, which had no eyelids, were very small in proportion to the body—about the size of a sheep's eyes.

The external portion of the ear was so small and well concealed that it was almost indistinguishable among the many grooves and wrinkles of the hide. Even when Steller removed the hide, the ear duct was noticeable only by its polished blackness, its opening hardly large enough to accommodate a pea. Although little is known about the hearing capabilities of Steller's sea cow, size should not be taken as an indication of hearing quality. Many of the larger marine mammals, specifically whales, have similar small openings but excellent hearing.

The back of the animal was shaped like that of an ox with a prominent middle backbone and flat hollows on both sides along the length of the back. The sides were round and the belly plump and "frog-like," although during the winter, the animals became so thin that their ribs would show. This observation, coupled with an exhaustive study of the evolution of the family of sirenians in the North Pacific, led paleontologist Daryl P. Domning to conclude that the Commander Islands area was a marginal habitat that didn't allow the sea cows to achieve their optimum growth despite the year-round availability of food. Still, the animals grew to a remarkable size.

Steller estimated the length of the largest animals at "4 to 5 fathoms," which, at 6 feet per fathom, would measure out to a maximum size of 30 feet; some scientists believe they could have been as large as 35 feet in length, although 26 feet seems to be the size generally accepted by paleontologists. The weight of a full-grown adult has been a point of debate ever since Steller gave two conflicting accounts, writing at one time an estimate of "200 pud," or 4.5 tons, and at another "1,200 pud," or 26.8 tons. Paleontologists believe that 10 tons is a more realistic estimate based on skeletal structure and a comparison to living cetaceans of similar body length and girth, such as orcas.

Along with their great size, sea cows had a very thick black or dark brown hide up to an inch thick, with "a consistency almost like cork, around the head full of grooves, wrinkles, and holes." This distinctive skin cover, which together with the blubber layer kept the animal warm and acted as a "collision mat" for swimming in shallow, rocky water, gives the sea cow its German popular name *Borkentier*, the "bark animal."

Besides its bizarre appearance, Steller's sea cow exhibited a variety of peculiar characteristics that show it was highly adapted to its northern coastal environment. Anyone who has ever been in the water with manatees knows that they exhibit tremendous buoyancy control, moving up and down effortlessly with no apparent exertion. This is due to several physiological characteristics, from skeletal structure to the location of their diaphragms. However, Steller's sea cow was so buoyant it rarely, if ever, submerged. Steller, and several of the hunters that followed after him, reported that fully half of the body projected so high above the water that seagulls would perch upon their backs and leisurely pick off the vermin that infested sea cow skin. Apparently when the animals rested, they would choose a quiet cove, roll over on their backs, and float lazily, riding the ocean swells like gigantic logs.

Although this type of buoyancy would appear to be a disadvantage, in truth it had several benefits. Floating with their backs high above water enabled them to feed in shallow areas and escape from deepwater predators. It also allowed sea birds to remove parasites and reduced conductive heat loss while increasing exposure to the heat of the sun. It may have even reduced wave drag as they swam.

Lieutenant Sven Waxell, Bering's second-in-command and an experienced seaman, also noticed that the sea cows always faced into the current, much like ships riding out a storm. This swimming posture allowed them to maintain steering control in the tumultuous waves and powerful tides of the area while the flexibility of their necks enabled them to crop plants on either side. When control was lost, their tough hide protected them against serious scrapes.

Despite the fact that *Hydrodamalis gigas* was never reported to submerge, Domning believes that the ability to dive under adverse conditions was too important a capability to have been totally lost. Instead, he suggests that "unlike any other known marine mammal, floating was the preferred posture for normal activity."

Although they never showed any fear of human beings, which is not surprising given their remote environment, sea cows undoubtedly had predators, most likely killer whales and large sharks. Steller noted in his journal that the young animals were always kept in the middle of the herd. Their ability to retreat to extremely shallow water strewn with rocks would make them difficult prey for ocean-going predators. Their unusual buoyancy would have also made them a difficult catch for killer whales, who often drown air-breathing prey by repeatedly breaching on their backs to force them underwater.

Sea cows also demonstrated a strong protective instinct for each other, not only for calves. Steller noted in his journal:

When an animal caught with the hook began to move
about somewhat violently,those nearest in the herd began
to stir also and feel the urge to bring succor. To this end
some of them tried to upset the boat with their backs,

while others pressed down the rope and endeavored to break it, or strove to remove the hook from the wound in the back by blows of their tail, in which they actually succeeded several times. It is a most remarkable proof of their conjugal affection that the male, after having tried with all his might, although in vain, to free the female caught by the hook, and in spite of the beating we gave him, nevertheless followed her to shore, and that several times, even after she was dead, he shot unexpectedly up to her like a speeding arrow. Early next morning, when we came to cut up the meat and bring it to the dugout, we found the male again standing by the female, and the same I observed once more on the third day when I went there myself for the sole purpose of examining the intestines.

As the summer wore on, Steller had numerous opportunities to analyze the anatomy of this remarkable creature. On July 12, he dissected a large female that had been dragged ashore. The heart alone weighed over 36 pounds. The stomach was large, about 6 feet long and 5 feet wide, and so stuffed with food that four men were barely able to pull the organ out with a rope. But it wasn't long before Steller's assistants, now strengthened from their high-quality diet, lost interest in their work and "from ignorance and disgust would tear everything out in pieces, and acted according to their own inclinations," despite the fact that Steller was now paying them with tobacco, an item that had taken the place of money. Together with the unceasing rain and cold, temperatures and the packs of aggressive Arctic foxes, Steller's studies grew increasingly difficult. Yet he persisted, even to the point of having six accurate renderings drawn to scale by the expedition draftsman.

In August 1742, the shipwrecked explorers finally completed the construction of the ship and departed Bering Island, named after their deceased leader, who had succumbed to illness on the desolate shore. After arriving safely in Petropavlovsk on the Kamchatka Peninsula, Steller forwarded his findings to St. Petersburg. He died four years later in Siberia at the age of thirty-seven before his writings were ever published. Today he is recognized as one of the world's early scientific geniuses whose skills embraced biology, enthnography, and medicine. His observations of four large North Pacific sea mammals—the fur seal, the sea otter, the sea lion, and the sea cow—set the standard for the day and remain the only scientific record of the living sea cow. His notes were so accurate, so painstakingly thorough, despite the often brutal conditions, that when the United States took possession of the Pribilof Islands in the mid-nineteenth century, government scientists who studied the herds of fur seals there made no changes in Steller's description of the species.

After the return of the expedition, exploitation of the resources of the Commander Islands began in earnest. At the time of their discovery, it is estimated that there were as many as two thousand sea cows around Bering and Copper islands. Amazingly, it took only twenty-seven years to eradicate the last of them.

Typical of the practices of the fur hunters, who were most responsible for the destruction of the sea cow herds, is this account from the diary of a mining engineer, Petr Yakovlev, who wintered on Bering Island in 1754–1755:

How the hunting of those cows was carried out then, was observed in the so-called Nizovtsovaya Harbor, since there in the sea near the shore can always be observed [at least] one [sea cow], and those cows go in herds. For hunting them, about eight men ride in a whaleboat, one of which has a long rod on which is attached a wide and long strip of pointed metal [*pokolyuga*], with which he stands near the stern in front of the steersman, and the others sit at the oars and when they reach alongside the head of the cow and the standing one with the *pokolyuga* gives a hearty wound to that sea beef, and the rowers with the whaleboat have to hurriedly row away from the cow so that that stabbed sea cow would not break up their whaleboat with its tail as well as with its flipper. And thus this stabbed beef, with a hearty wound not swimming for long in the sea, becomes exhausted and stopping at a spot turns its belly upward. And from the same cows the removed skins are utilized in the manufactures of baydars [skin boats], in which it is quite comfortable to travel at sea, better than the wooden whaleboat; also for the manufacture of footwear and they are also used for the soles for it.

Other accounts tell of wasteful killing. Sea cows were so easy to kill that a patient man armed only with a spear could wade into the water, stab the animal and simply wait for the terrified creature to exhaust itself, die, then wash ashore. Many of the creatures killed this way, however, were lost as they drifted out with the outgoing tide. Even at the time of Yakovlev's visit, the herds were starting to disappear, especially around Copper Island. He notes this in his diary, sounding a cautionary note: "One could find thousands of sea otter and herds of sea cows, but now these cows are so eradicated that never does one see even one, in such a state does this Mednyy Island [Copper Island] now actually exist, that there are no longer any herds of cows near it."

Just over a decade later, in 1786, a hunter named Ivan Popov thrust his lance into what has purported to be the last Great Northern sea cow ever captured, ending a remarkably brutal and efficient hunt and robbing the earth of one of its most intriguing creatures. In the centuries since, scientists of many nationalities have debated the continued existence of the animal. The seas in that area are vast, the coasts barren and desolate. Could a population of sea cows have existed in other parts of the Bering Sea during Steller's time? Can an isolated herd still live somewhere? Perhaps the answers lie in the evolutionary trail of *Hydrodamalis gigas.*

Steller's sea cow is descended from smaller tropical sea cows that once flourished off the coast of Peru. Over the course of 20 million years of evolution, the ancestors of *Hydrodamalis gigas* gradually adapted to feeding primarily on kelps, which thrive in the colder, more turbulent waters of the North Pacific. Their larger body size and thicker skin and blubber were adaptations that conserved heat and protected them as they fed off exposed, rocky shores. At its maximum, their range once extended from northern Mexico around the coasts of the North Pacific to the Japanese archipelago. As recently as twenty thousand years ago they still swam off central California. With the coming of man in the Pleistocene epoch, however, the range of the tasty sea cows began to diminish until it was limited, not coincidentally, to the two uninhabited islands that Steller and his comrades were stranded on a mere 250 years ago. Put simply, the paleontological trail points quite clearly to man as the prime culprit for the extinction of Steller's sea cow, a process that actually began with native coastal hunters centuries before Steller's appearance on those barren, lonely islands. As for the existence of an isolated population off some other uninhabited island in the North Pacific, there have been a few sightings reported since 1768, including several in this century. For example, in 1910 there was a report of a dead sea cow washing up at Cape Chaplin in the northern part of the Gulf of Anadyr in the northwest section of the Bering Sea. However, the Soviet Scientific Institute of Fisheries and Oceanographic Research in the Pacific never seriously considered such reports from the fishermen of the region and chose instead to ignore the incident. Yet a sighting in 1962 by the crew of the whaler *Buran*, near Cape Navarin in the southern portion of the same gulf, caused a sensation.

It was early on a July morning as the Buran cruised the waters just off the Cape when the men on watch were startled by the sighting of a half-dozen bizarre-looking animals swimming 80 to 100 yards away. They were unlike any cetacean or pinniped the experienced whalers had ever seen. The creatures varied in length from 20 to 26 feet, with dark skin and small heads with overlapping split upper lips. They swam slowly in a compact group, occasionally diving for brief periods before surfacing in a very distinctive manner. Their tails, which were seen as they dove, were edged with fringe. Interestingly enough, the same animals were sighted the next morning nearby in a shallow lagoon where sea kale and seaweed flourished.

The creatures were remarkable for their similarities to Steller's sea cows, especially in the distinctive head and tail. In addition, the shallow coastal environment was ideal and the color and size of the animals an appropriate match. The only other creature in that region with such a peculiar snout would be a walrus, yet they rarely grow over 13 feet in length and most certainly would have been easily recognized by the experienced hunters aboard the Buran.

The Russian naturalists, A. A. Berzin, E. A. Tikhomirov, and V. I. Troinin investigated the sightings and recorded these comments in *Priroda* [nature], a publication of the Academy of Sciences of the USSR:

As we know, the sea-cow was completely exterminated in the Komandorski Islands by fur-seal hunters. However, in other areas, where the sea-cow may have lived, if we are to judge from the data cited, there was no hunting of this kind, because there were no animals with valuable fur.

We may suppose that the sea-cow could have survived there if adequate ecological conditions coincided, but we have no information on the subject. If this is the case, the sea-cow must have been able to remain unnoticed for a long time.

Domning was cautious in his comments on the sightings, theorizing instead that the animals may have been female narwhals which, although rare in the Bering Sea, have occasionally been sighted that far south. The difficulty with this hypothesis is that narwhals rarely grow over 16 feet in length, have smooth-edged flukes, and have distinctive spotting or mottling on their dorsal surface, which would make them fairly easy to identify, especially for experienced whalers. Domning does conclude, however, that the report was intriguing enough to warrant further investigation in the hopes of turning up some concrete evidence.

Another interesting report from a little earlier in this century was sent in a letter to the Scottish naturalist Ivan T. Sanderson by a Mrs. Charles Timeus of Wilmar, California, and reproduced in Bernard Heuvelmans' book *In the Wake of the Sea-Serpents*. In it she describes a creature that she and her husband sighted on a trip to British Columbia in 1937:

Returning from a fishing trip, toward sunset, pulling into
. . . Sunset Beach, 22 miles north of Vancouver, we saw a
huge Mammal or Monster not more than 25 feet from our
boat. It had a large head which resembled a long nosed
pig only wider at snout, two large flippers and huge body,
we watched it for several minutes, it did not seem alarmed
but stayed there until we were out on shore. We searched
the dictionary and the only thing we could find that
resembled it was a Manatee.

The letter goes on to describe a similar creature sighted by two brothers and a group of fishermen in the same location, with an estimated length of between 50 and 100 feet. Portions of the description match the features of a Steller's sea cow, although the estimated size is too large. Fishermen, however, have never been too reliable in reporting the size of their potential catch.

Nevertheless, accounts such as these, although not always submitted by experienced naturalists, contribute to the possibility, however remote, that somewhere out there, swimming near some remote uninhabited North Pacific island, is a remnant population of these incredible animals.

Rudyard Kipling wrote a fanciful tale in *The Jungle Books* collection of short stories, published in 1894 and 1895, on this very subject. In "The White Seal," a seal named Kotick is horrified when he witnesses the brutal slaughter of his companions at the hands of fur hunters in the Bering Sea. His white coat, which the hunters view as an unlucky omen, saves the seal, and shortly afterwards he begins a search for an island which will ensure a safe haven for all seals.

He first consults a sea lion who refers him to Sea Vitch, "the big, ugly, bloated, pimpled, fat-necked, long-tusked walrus of the North Pacific."

'Go and ask Sea Cow,' said Sea Vitch. 'If he is living still he'll be able to tell you.'

'How shall I know Sea Cow when I meet him?' said Kotick, sheering off.

'He's the only thing in the sea uglier than Sea Vitch,' screamed a burgomaster gull, wheeling under Sea Vitch's nose. 'Uglier, and with worse manners!'

For five seasons Kotick searches but does not find any sea cows, all the while hearing of the destruction of seal rookeries everywhere. Finally, he begins a search to the west, stopping to rest in the weed beds off Copper Island. During the night he's gently bumped awake by some huge animals browsing on the weeds there. He has found the sea cows, or rather they have found him.

His efforts to communicate with the huge mammals end in failure, so Kotick decides to track them as they migrate, in an attempt to find their secret haven.

For days he follows them as they move slowly north until suddenly, in the dark of the night, their pace quickens and they begin to sink like stones, heading for a hole in the base of a nearby cliff. After a long dive that leaves Kotick puffing and wheezing, they emerge into a protected harbor, far beyond the reach of hunters, where food is plentiful, beaches are beautiful, and ships bearing people can't land. Elated, Kotick returns to lead nearly ten thousand seals to the safe harbor "beyond Sea Cow's tunnel."

With this fanciful thought of a safe haven for sea cows, I took one last glance at the dusty bones hanging ignominiously in a corner of the Harvard museum and headed out into a cold, overcast November day in Cambridge. I wondered how many people ever gave more than a passing thought to the once grand creature whose remains adorned a forgotten corner of this massive building. The demise of the Steller's sea cows may not have had a dramatic impact on the earth's ecology; it does, however, offer an example of the finality of extinction and the danger of apathy. For within a few short decades, a creature refined by 20 million years of evolution vanished from the last place on earth that had offered refuge from the world's most relentless hunter—man. And all that remains to give them life are a few forgotten bony relics and the words of a youthful German naturalist.

AN UNCERTAIN FUTURE

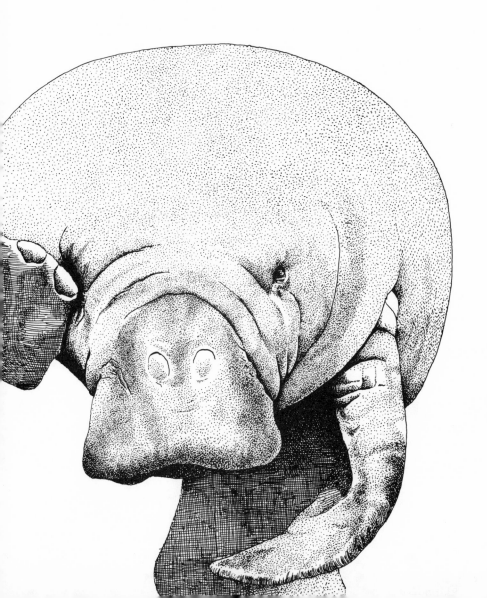

THE WATCHERS

Standing on a dock overlooking the broad expanse of the St. John's River, I felt as if I had discovered paradise. Below, bright sparkles of sunlight danced playfully off the ebony waters as ospreys and red-shouldered hawks soared in the rich blue skies overhead, their calls echoing in the still morning air. The river seemed alive at every glance. Otters surfaced and dove repeatedly as they made their way to shore. Here and there a fish broke the surface, tempting the black cormorants who eyed the activity from shoreside perches. Even the live oaks, their branches fingering skyward and draped with light gray moss, seemed to lend vitality to a primordial scene that stretched in both directions as far as I could see.

"This is a special time of day," said Wayne Hartley, jolting me out of my reverie. "I often come here early in the morning just to listen to the sounds and enjoy the solitude before the park opens." He glanced wistfully out over the water. "It's hard to believe that much of this is in danger and may change in our lifetime. But the possibility is there."

With that comment, he turned and motioned me toward a row of canoes lying keel-up on the bank of the river. There was work to be done, a special count to be taken, and he was eager to get going before the crowds started to arrive.

I had come to Orange City, Florida, a sleepy little town about 25 miles north of Orlando, to join Wayne, a ranger at Blue Spring State Park, on his winter morning count of manatees. Despite its distant inland location, Blue Spring Run is one of the most popular winter refuges for manatees, and few know these unusual winter guests better than my gracious host. He has been watching them closely since joining the park staff in 1979, providing written reports to his employer, the Florida DNR, as well as the U.S. Fish & Wildlife Service and the Save the Manatee Club in nearby Maitland. For many concerned with the plight of the manatees, he is their eyes and ears, even their conscience—a consummate naturalist who has more or less adopted the manatees as his charges. Dressed in a ranger uniform with its crisp, pleated trousers and distinctive "Smokey" hat, Wayne is everyone's idea of a park ranger, the epitome of the stereotypical, almost mythical, hero of the woods and streams. His jaw may not be so square and his hair may be flecked with gray and growing just a tad thin, but everything else is there: the quick, ready smile, the infinite patience, and, most importantly, true dedication and commitment to the task at hand—saving manatees.

"It may be getting a bit too breezy to get a completely accurate count," said Wayne, pointing to the wind-whipped ripples streaming across the water's surface. "But I think once we maneuver down under those oaks we'll be out of the direct wind."

"I couldn't help but notice this sign here warning about alligators," I said as matter-of-factly as possible, while flipping the canoe over onto its keel near the water's weedy edge. "Do you really ever see any around here?"

He shrugged. "Oh sure. There's been a few in the run from time to time."

I stepped gingerly into the canoe as we shoved off. For some reason I was compelled to keep my hands from dangling in the water, at least until we worked our way into the clear waters upstream.

On a tree branch not 10 feet overhead, an osprey eyed us suspiciously, following our movements with quick jerks of its head and the cold, staring eyes of a predator. As we maneuvered around the buoys marking off the entrance to the run, the water rapidly lost its black, swamp-water coloring and turned a brilliant aquamarine hue with drinking-water clarity and more fish and manatees than I had ever seen gathered in one spot. They had come, as they had for untold millenia, to spend the winter in the water that surges to the surface in the Blue Spring boil just about a third of a mile up the run. The manatees don't come because the water is beautiful; nor do they come because it's the place to see or be seen mate-wise. The draw is the constant 72 degree temperature of the water, which allows these tropical mammals to survive the occasional cold spells of a Florida winter.

Blue Spring is a spectacular natural feature resulting from rainwater seeping through sandy soil and porous limestone bedrock deep into the ground, where it is protected from daily and seasonal fluctuations in temperature. As it makes its way back to the sea, the water flows through subterranean limestone caverns and tunnels, eventually surging to the surface at the Blue Spring boil at the rate of 100 million gallons a day. Its narrow course down the short Run to the St. John's River provides an important winter refuge for over sixty manatees.

Prior to the establishment of the park as a refuge in 1972, swimmers used the boil as a party ground, chasing and riding the few manatees who dared return each year. When the state took over the run, the rangers found animals that had been stabbed and beaten. Some even had old ropes tied on them from previous riders. Now, however, it's the manatees who have priority, and during the winter months, when they move into the portion of the run accessible to people, it's the swimmers and divers who must leave. For this reason, Blue Spring is the antithesis of Crystal River, where manatees outside the sanctuaries are fully accessible.

During my many visits to the park, I've always been struck by the reverence the setting seems to engender in people. The unspoiled scenery and the remarkable abundance of wildlife, along with the almost magical hue of the water, provide a refreshing respite from the hectic, fast-paced glitz of the massive Florida theme parks located only a few miles away. Strolling along the hidden boardwalk, which winds along the full distance of the run, the first thing you notice is that everyone whispers. There are no signs requesting quiet, nor is there a need for the rangers to shush raucous revelers. Everyone whispers simply because it seems like the right thing to do, as if worshipping in a cathedral of nature. Making loud, abrasive noises seems blasphemous.

Life at the spring moves at a sane, more purposeful pace. Sleeping manatees lie like large gray slugs on the shallow, sandy bottom, rising every few minutes to catch a quick breath. Skimmers and hawks cut and weave irregular airy paths as they dodge the moss-draped branches overhanging the water. And more fish than could fill a fisherman's dream loop in lazy circles below the overlooks: Florida gars, longnose gars, striped bass, largemouth bass, sunfish, mullett, bluegills, snook, even an occasional tarpon. This is Florida at its natural best: a vital, pulsing, natural oasis offering vivid proof of the power of protection.

It was in this setting that Wayne and I paddled out to meet his extended "family." Out of the 125 or so manatees that have visited Blue Spring over the past dozen years, there's nary a one that Wayne hasn't become personally familiar with. He knows many of them as well as you or I might know our brothers and sisters. Although the propeller scars are his principle means of identification, he is also tuned to each idiosyncrasy, any subtle nuance that might give him a clue even before he sees the scars.

In a melodious southern accent, he said, "Brutus, you've got so many scars on you it's hard to tell if you've got a new one." A large adult, its back riddled with a series of crosscut gashes and one long slice caused by a boat propeller, glided under the canoe.

"Is that you, Deep Dent?" he asked of an equally large adult, this one a known male, as it materialized beneath the rippled waters just in front of our canoe. "This guy has large deep dents that go all the way through his tail, so it wasn't difficult to decide on his name."

I noticed that each time Wayne recognized an animal, he dropped his oar and made a notation on a chart that divides the entire run into nineteen small sections called vegetation transects. He scribbled a little dot accompanied by a number, each of which represents a particular animal. These notes later help him in drawing up a master spotting chart for the day showing which animals were in the spring and in what section they were sighted. On that still winter morning, it seemed like all the animals were gathered in the front three sections near the mouth of the run.

"That's Luke," said Wayne confidently, as a chubby, bewhiskered face glanced up from the port side. "He's a yearling from last year who's been weaned already. At least that's who I hope he is. When a calf isn't too scarred and gets weaned early it's difficult." Suddenly Wayne pointed off the starboard side. "That's Crazy Nick. And there's Milton, though I can't get close enough to be sure."

Manatees were all around us, popping up to and fro, snorting loudly as they cleared their nostrils for great sniffs of air. Wayne was clearly energized by the swirl of bodies that moved through the greenish-blue water below. "Luna," he called to a large female moving rapidly to our right, as if he were addressing a neighbor next door. "Where's your baby?" He laughed pleasantly as he gently chided the new mother whose calf was not in sight. "Luna, go find your baby!"

"Who's that animal over there?" I asked, pointing to the water ahead of the canoe, where several huge scars on the back of a large adult glowed white beneath the sun-dappled surface.

"Oh, that's Sweetgums. She's the mother of the one in the middle, which we've named O'Shea. As you can see, he's pretty big for a yearling calf," he whispered as the mother-son duo nestled quietly into the shallow, still waters beneath an overhanging oak. "Sweetgums was the center of an estrous herd a while ago. Every time she would leave to eat, the run would empty because most of the manatees here are male. Then the visitors would ask us where all the manatees were. Well, they were all chasing Sweetgums. She thought it was great!"

Our discussion was suddenly interrupted by a ranger calling from the observation platform on the other side of the run. "Wayne!" he yelled through cupped hands. "These folks here have adopted Phillip. Have you seen him today?"

"I haven't seen him yet. But I've got a lot more to go."He paused for a moment then added as an afterthought, "He has been in the spring during this latest cold spell, though."

One of Wayne's volunteer duties is to provide updates on the individual manatees found at the spring for the Save the Manatee Club and its adoption program. By paying a nominal fee, you can "adopt" a manatee of your choice from a list provided by the Club. In return, you receive a brief life history of your manatee as well as a glossy black-and-white photo. The money helps to promote public awareness about the endangered mammals while supporting the Club's conservation efforts. At the park, Wayne is the source of information on all the manatees and is the first person anyone asks for updates on their whereabouts.

An area as high and dry as Fort Worth, Texas, is an unusual place for a manatee expert to hail from, but like many of the people drawn to work with marine mammals, Wayne's fascination with manatees started when he was only a boy, and curiosity had more to do with his developing interest than with location. "My grandmother gave me a book on North American wildlife back in 1953," he recalled, halting his note-taking for a moment. "I was flipping through the book and came to a picture of a manatee. When I saw the photo my reaction was 'Good grief! This thing exists in America?' I thought animals like that lived only in exotic places like Antarctica or the jungles of Africa, not in the United States." As the years passed, Wayne ended up working as a ranger in Florida and was eventually assigned to Blue Spring. At the time, federal and university researchers were conducting telemetry studies on the population of manatees at the spring to document their seasonal movements. Fascinated, Wayne volunteered to come in early to assist with the study, and he gradually learned many of the techniques necessary for providing accurate data. When federal budget cuts dried up funds for the study, Wayne was asked to maintain an annual count of manatees on his own, a responsibility he relishes today under the auspices of his employer, the Florida DNR, the state agency that oversees the protection of manatees.

Our discussion was interrupted by the appearance of a manatee that rose within inches of the canoe, its snout caked sloppily with a white substance that looked like frosting.

"They eat clay sometimes and get all white around the muzzle," noted Wayne, pushing his paddle down off the stern to stop our forward progress. Suddenly he flashed a smile. "Oh look!" he chuckled. "There's Wayne Hartley, the Second!"

"You mean they've named one after you?" I asked, as a medium-size manatee sporting some small propeller hash marks on its rear dorsal surface nosed its way in our direction.

He waved his hand as if to brush off the honor. "Yeah," he said, somewhat embarrassed. "A few years ago, somebody said, 'When are we going to name one after Wayne?' At the time I was using a system where I'd name them WH1 and WH2 and so on as I saw them. The WH let the people reading the reports know that I was the one who had sighted the animals. The number helped me distinguish which one was which. So, thanks to Tom O'Shea, who came up with the idea, WH2 became Wayne Hartley, the Second."

Dr. Tom O'Shea is the Sirenia Project leader for the U.S. Fish & Wildlife Service's National Ecology Research Center in Gainesville, a group that was established in the 1970s to focus on long-term biological research. Wayne's reports augment the group's manatee life-history research and scar-pattern catalog, the federal agency's ongoing record of the state's manatees. Each note, every sketch of a new scar, is sent to Gainesville to update the records.

As we maneuvered the canoe through a maze of overhanging oak branches, struggling occasionally against brief gusts of wind that threatened to send us headlong into a submerged manatee, I was amazed by the dexterous movements of the gray behemoths below us, any one of which outweighed Wayne and me and the canoe put together. Although only inches away, not one of them even came close to disturbing our craft. However, a couple of the larger adults started to show more than a passing interest in us, which seemed to make Wayne a bit uncomfortable.

"Shoot," he said in an exasperated tone. "I encourage this curiosity by hanging around them. They're getting too accustomed to the boat. You'll notice I carry waterproof equipment." He held up a collection of pads and pencils wrapped in plastic. "We were knocked out of the canoe once when we startled one of the animals. Howie was in a cavorting group with several others and was pretty close to the boat. He's around us so much we didn't think much about it until we accidently bumped him. When we hit, it surprised him because he didn't know we were there. He panicked and lunged forward to escape, which of course sent the canoe rocking one way. Then he dove, flipping his tail up, which knocked us back the other way. That's when we all rolled out of the canoe."

I looked at all my camera equipment and the tape recorder and admonished myself for not preparing for a possible dunking. At that point we had drifted into the midst of eight to ten resting animals, so Wayne tapped on the side of the canoe to alert them to our position. The noise brought a couple of curious snouts to the gunwales. Affectionately, Wayne reached out to scratch the grizzled muzzle of a particularly curious female with a set of deep propeller slashes on the dorsal surface in the area where her wide body narrowed toward the tail.

"Look, here's Dana!" he said excitedly. "I haven't seen her for quite some time."

The attention was clearly appreciated as Dana willingly held her position next to Wayne. As soon as he stopped scratching, she disappeared beneath the surface with a "plurping" sound.

If there is one dramatically visible sign of man's effect on the manatees at Blue Spring, it was the embarrassing amount of scars and mutilation visible on each animal. Forget the fact that every animal we saw that day, a total of thirty-seven, had scars. The sad part was that most of them had several scars. A few were even horribly disfigured. No Tail, a large male first seen at the spring in 1983, lost over 80 percent of his tail in a collision with a boat propeller. Phoebe was one of the first animals to be identified at Blue Spring in 1971. Besides carrying a plethora of propeller slashes on the rear portion of her dorsal surface, she has lost the use of her left front flipper which became entangled in discarded monofilament line, resulting in a constricted appendage. The injury, however, hasn't cramped her style, as she is purported to be one of the most prolific mothers at the spring, producing at least six calves in the last two decades. At the time of my visit, she was sporting a new 18-inch gash all the way through her tail. But the true survivor of all the manatees in the run is Success. She was resting close to the north bank about 20 feet from our canoe. At that distance, with the water distorting her ample figure, she looked more like a giant scar than a manatee. Wayne just whistled and shook his head in amazement.

"That's Success. We named her that because she was a successful calf of Sweetgums, who previously had so many stillbirths. One time, when we were out radio tracking Sweetgums, we found Success swimming nearby with so much meat ripped out of her she looked deformed. It was an optical illusion. Did you ever see a crooked fish? That's what she looked like, only her backbone was straight. Anyway, she came back in with this horrible wound and it eventually healed. Then we saw her again with another boat hit right over the one she had, only this time there were bones sticking out of her sides. Two were very prominent. People would come in to report a manatee with sticks stuck in it, but they weren't sticks, they were bones. As time went by, flesh grew out to cover them. Now she has a ball of flesh that just sort of sticks up."

As Wayne continued his story, I watched the disfigured animal move slowly across the sandy bottom of the run.

"Initially her growth wasn't too good, so we were afraid she had a disease of the backbone, which manatees sometimes get when they're badly maimed."

He pointed at her oddly shaped tail, which looked more like a dugong's fluke than a manatee's tail, and added, "A year later she came back with a v-shaped notch taken out of the end of her tail. It looked like she was trying to impersonate a dugong. Year after year we figure out another reason why she ought to die. But she just goes on. Manatees can take a lot of punishment."

According to Wayne, Success then became more than a tribute to the survival instinct. She became a mother. In 1989, she returned to Blue Spring with a calf, appropriately named Destiny.

As we paddled upstream, we found a large group of manatees gathered in the shade of an ancient oak tree, its large moss-covered branches spread like an umbrella over the water. Just off to the port side, Wayne pointed to a submerged trunk of a sable palm tree, which several of the animals hovered around.

"That's their rubbing log. They love to chew it, rub it, and push it around," he added while setting the oar down to make a few notes on the animals lounging near the spot. "There's plenty of logs they could fool with, but most of them return to the same log year after year. I think it's like a calling card they leave their taste or smell on for the others to find. At Crystal River there are certain rocks they treat the same way."

Wayne's hunch, while not a proven fact, may very well be close to the truth. Throughout their range, manatees, especially female, have been known to rub themselves against logs, rocks, ropes, and even the hulls of boats, using the parts of their bodies that produce glandular secretions, such as the areas around the genitals, the eyes, the base of their pectoral fins, and the chin. Although manatees are very tactile creatures and this may simply be a way to relieve itching, some researchers speculate that in rubbing inanimate objects they are leaving a message, perhaps involving a scent of some kind, concerning their receptiveness to reproduction.

Wayne looked down at his note pad. "Let's see, I haven't seen Boomer and I haven't seen June or Phyllis," he noted as we moved up the run toward the boil. "These are the animals I expect to find in this area of the run, nearer the swimming area. This is sort of their favorite spot."

We tacked back and forth across the width of the run, pausing at every sighting to make a note or take a photo. Most of the manatees were gathered near the bank on the north side of the run beneath the trees, probably to avoid the steady current that flowed out toward the St. John's. We moved up toward the swimming area, where the water was a little more shallow and exposed. There we found Judith, Julie, and finally, as Wayne had predicted, June.

"There she is," motioned Wayne with a note of triumph. "See those two white spots on her sides? She's just gotten those. She's only three, and every year it gets harder to identify her because her other scars have healed completely without leaving any clear marks.

All young manatees heal quickly, but June heals quicker than most."

"It seems like there are plenty of scars on all these animals," I replied, pointing out the obvious. "Certainly enough to identify each of them."

"Oh yeah. The young ones get about twelve nonfatal propeller hits each year—that's an average. When Tom [O'Shea] was in one day he counted all the scars on a sampling of young animals in the run. The two- and three-year-olds averaged about thirty-six. And he was careful to avoid counting numerous scars from a single hit. Humans would be in the hospital for weeks getting stitched up. But for manatees, it's normal."

After years of underwater and surface encounters with scores of manatees, I could recall only one that didn't have some sort of propeller scar. The vast majority of manatees in Florida carry several of them. And it isn't difficult to understand why. I remembered renting a canoe at the Park a few years before to explore a portion of the St. John's. It proved to be a harrowing experience, graphically illustrating the problem of too many boats and too few protected waterways. As I paddled upriver, boats rounded a blind corner at full throttle, their inboard props roaring and set deep off the stern, throwing massive wakes that threatened to flip my fragile craft. This despite large red and white signs that declared in highly visible letters: "Idle Speed—Manatee Area." Once the owners of these power craft rounded the corner and saw me in my green canoe and khaki-colored shirt, which bore enough of a resemblance to the uniform of a park ranger or a Marine Patrol officer to give them a start, they'd let up on the throttle and idle down so that the huge wake that swelled up off their stern threatened to swamp them instead of me. Then it was all smiles and waves.

I decided to carry the ruse a little farther and rowed up to a raft of hyacinths in a tributary that was visible only when you were even with the mouth. I sat there looking very official, pointing my long telephoto lens directly at the offenders. I enjoyed the flurry of activity that resulted when the driver or one of his passengers glimpsed me in position and thought they had been caught in the act. I suspect I gave more than a few heart flutters to a lot of careless boaters.

Unfortunately, manatees don't have such policing capabilities. Indeed, their basic character trait is unflinching docility. Their gentle demeanor is so inherent in one and all that, at first, it's hard to distinguish one from another. Canoeing directly over the resting mammals with Wayne, they all seemed to act and look alike, with the exception of the scars. But to the experienced eye, they are indeed different, each has a distinctive personality. Deep Dent does not like the canoe and will swim away when approached. Phoebe is the grande dame of all, a fertile female who is often accompanied by an entourage of suitors and offspring. Unlike many manatee mothers, Phoebe will not allow extended nursing and won't even consider nursing another's calf. She weans her own offspring after a year and there's no looking back. Boomer likes people and is very amiable and easy to approach. Sweetgums likes to hang out in marinas, putting herself and her offspring in danger but stubbornly returning to the same spots each year.

To Wayne, the manatees of Blue Spring are more than animals; they're friends. And when they don't return for an extended period of time, he worries like a father whose daughters are out on their first date. Still, in observing manatees year after year one has to deal with a lot of tragedy, and the acceptance of death, however difficult, is a part of the job.

"The DNR has a volume thick with photos of dead manatees from the period in 1990 immediately after the deep freeze," commented Wayne, recalling the aftermath of a particularly vicious cold spell in December 1989, which killed at least forty-six, possibly as many as seventy-five manatees. "There were so many dead manatees those poor people were just snowed under. Four of ours may have been among them."

The gusty wind made maneuvering the canoe difficult as we crossed to the southern side of the run. Most of the manatees had settled down and there was little surface activity other than an occasional snort as an animal stole to the surface for a quick breath. As we rested for a moment, our conversation turned to the length of the manatee sighting season at Blue Spring.

"The regulars usually start arriving around mid-November when the St. John's River temperature drops to about sixty-eight degrees. That's the magic number! When it hits sixty-eight they'll be drifting in all day long. It's that predictable! The season usually ends sometime in March, but it's not unusual to have manatees in the run in April. It really depends on the weather. I remember once we had about fourteen or fifteen young manatees hanging around even though the river had just warmed up. I was out there in the canoe saying, 'Y'all must know something I don't if you're staying around here.' Sure enough, we had two days of frost. Soon as it warmed up, they were gone."

During the summer months, the manatees who winter at Blue Spring spread out all along the St. John's up toward Jacksonville and along the north and central portions of Florida's east coast. Although there is still much to be learned about their summer migration patterns, manatees are capable of traveling great distances, as evidenced by none other than Wayne's namesake, Wayne Hartley II. He has been sighted four times swimming 700 to 800 river miles south of Blue Spring off the Coral Gables/Miami area, the farthest confirmed distance traveled by a Blue Spring manatee.

Wayne's efforts help researchers from the Sirenia Project, the Marine Research Laboratory (DNR), and Beaufort Laboratory (National Marine Fisheries Service) in their statewide efforts to learn more about the seasonal movements of manatees through the use of satellite-monitored transmitters, aerial surveys, the ongoing study of winter aggregations like those at Blue Spring, and food habits analysis.

Every year when manatees return to winter aggregation sites, many to the same sites year after year, each is identified by its unique scar patterns. Through long-term observation, and the maintenance of thousands of photographs on file, researchers are gradually unlocking the many secrets of manatee behavior and ecology such as reproductive habits, seasonal movements, habitat usage, and the dynamics of family groupings.

Much of what is known about the seasonal movements of manatees came with the development of radio tracking. By attaching an electronic transmitter to a manatee, researchers with specially tuned receivers can locate the animal at a distance, pinpoint its location, and visually monitor its movements and behavior. The transmitters float at or near the surface of the water, attached by a 6-foot tether to a belt looped around the manatee's tail. If snagged, the units pop off as a safety precaution for the animal. A special link in the loop is designed to corrode so that the belt will eventually drop off once it is no longer useful. Some transmitters even transmit signals to satellites passing overhead, providing ongoing readouts on the complex movements of manatees in highly populated coastal areas. Satellite telemetry is the most efficient method of tracking but also the most expensive; a single transmitter can cost as much as five thousand dollars.

Initial results from the various methods of study show that some seasonal habitat use and movement patterns in eastern Florida vary dramatically from those on the Gulf Coast. Movements on the east coast, for example, seem much more extensive. In the summer, some east coast manatees favor specific portions of the Georgia coast and the Merritt Island National Wildlife Refuge on the central Atlantic coast of Florida, frequently traveling the 155 miles of coastal waterways connecting these two spots. Manatees also seem to favor quiet areas and large bodies of water where boating is prohibited, such as the waters around the Kennedy Space Center. According to Dr. O'Shea, individual animals retain migration patterns from year to year, possibly passing on the knowledge of routes from female to offspring. The findings clearly show that manatees will find and use sanctuaries, a fact that agrees with Wayne's personal observations.

"The thing that I think might turn it around for manatees is public education, lower speed limits for boats, and the establishment of summer refuges," he said, as we drifted slowly toward the mouth of the run, watching several of his charges glide beneath the canoe. "We've got some winter refuges, and we know they're used. We started with eleven manatees here in 1970 and now we're up to around sixty-three in the course of a year. When counts were first taken at Crystal River they had fifty or sixty animals, and now they've got close to three hundred. Why? Because they made a nice place and manatees realize this and prefer it. Manatees are showing up in greater numbers at the summer refuge next to Cape Canaveral because the habitat is good and boats are banned for national security reasons. Now what we've got to do is establish summer refuges, with no boats allowed, here and there up and down the coast. Of course, boaters don't like to be banned from anywhere, and fishermen don't like it a lot because good manatee habitat is also excellent for fishing. But if we want to save manatees we have to make the choices."

Glancing up at the growing crowd of people appearing on the boardwalk, I asked Wayne if he has seen an increase in concern for manatees during his years at the park.

He chuckled softly, gesturing toward a group pointing excitedly at Phoebe as she drifted near the overlook. "When I first came here, sometimes we'd get four hundred people on a week day and six hundred or so on a Saturday or Sunday, and we thought that was terrific. Now you might have two or three thousand on a Saturday or Sunday. We're closing the gates early because there's no more parking by mid-day."

Over the years, one of the things I've noticed repeatedly during my week-day visits to Blue Spring is the presence of large groups of schoolchildren. I asked Wayne about all the school buses in the parking lot.

"The schoolchildren who come here during the winter leave with a real feeling for manatees because most of them have gone through a lot of instruction even before they come. Most of these schools are really trying to make a difference. They care. Hopefully, it'll stick with the children. Then maybe they won't grow up and decide, 'Gee, I'd rather buy a cigarette boat and run eighty and turn my radio up so I can entertain everyone for miles around.'"

Boat speeds, and the need for regulations, is of particular importance to Wayne. For him, it's an issue that goes beyond saving the manatees. "Forty-seven manatees were killed by boats on our waterways in 1990," he noted grimly. "In the first ten months of that same year ninety-one people were also killed in boating accidents."

He rolled his eyes at the irony of the statistics, then continued. "Judith Delaney Vallee of the Save the Manatee Club commissioned a survey of boaters by an independent organization and the results were fantastic. It clearly showed that the majority of boaters are upset with what's going on. They're afraid for their lives out there. They want something done. It's the vocal minority that have the big boats and want to go fast. Most boaters want operator's licenses and speed limits. They're tired of going out for a relaxing day on the river and ending up fearing for their lives instead."

He grimaced, shaking his head. "We're going to get various boat speed regulations. We *are* going to get them. And it most likely will have nothing at all to do with manatees."

We rounded the buoys marking the entrance to the run and landed the canoe with a gentle thud, balancing carefully as we stepped out onto the muddy bank. We had seen thirty-seven regulars on the morning count, all of whom now seemed bunched up under the oaks near the mouth of the run, apparently in an effort to avoid the chop of the open water. Wayne seemed pleased to have seen so many familiar faces, each of them safe from the dangers and uncertainty of the open river. Now it was time to spread the message.

The pervading murmur of crowds with cameras, picnic baskets, and excited children in tow had replaced the gentle echoes of the early morning. As soon as we had off-loaded all our equipment, Wayne was immediately swept up in the hum of activity as people began peppering him with questions about manatees. Although he had probably heard the same questions thousands of times, his smile was engaging and sincere, and his answers full of the enthusiasm of a man on a mission. For him, each individual is another convert, another link to a new generation of hope for an endangered species. He seemed particularly animated when a group of schoolchildren gathered near the lecture hall in anticipation of his upcoming talk. I melted into the background as a tangle of chattering youngsters surrounded him. He glanced in my direction, winked, and said with a wide grin, "This is where it all starts." Moments later, he disappeared into the hall followed by the next generation of hope. For him, it's a story that never ends.

As I left Blue Spring, cars were lined up at the front gate for a good distance down the road and around the corner. It looked like business as usual. I began a journey south toward West Palm Beach to attend a manatee workshop given by Dr. J. Ross Wilcox, chief ecologist for Florida Power and Light Company (FPL), who works on behalf of both the manatees and the utility giant that provides winter refuge for a large majority of these endangered mammals.

Before the workshop we met in the lobby of a West Palm Beach hotel to discuss FPL's highly visible role in publicizing the plight of the manatee. Dr. Wilcox is a slight, bespectacled man with thinning brown hair and a clipped, halting style of speech that gives the impression that deep thought goes into every statement. He looks more like a lifetime academic than a representative for one of the country's largest and most powerful utilities. But, as I was to find out, there are many things about FPL that contradict the traditional image of a sprawling corporate giant.

With nine fossil-fuel plants and four nuclear units supplying power to almost two-thirds of the population of Florida, FPL is the fifth largest utility in the United States. Mega-corporations have never been considered friends of the environment, especially not companies operating nuclear power plants, and for many years the perception of FPL was no different. In the early 1980s, the company's chairman, Marshall McDonald, declared that FPL was operating "in a hostile environment, and for the first time, in a survival mode." Energy prices were skyrocketing, customer dissatisfaction was high, and construction costs on new facilities were escalating out of control. Then, in the mid-1980s, the company announced that it was embracing the philosophy of the American quality guru, W. Edwards Deming, whose precept "quality reaps rewards" played an integral role in rebuilding Japan into a world-class economic power after World War II. In a remarkable turnaround that left industry experts shaking their heads in amazement, FPL restructured and rebuilt an organization based on an unrelenting commitment to quality in less than half a decade. The effort culminated in FPL being the first American company to win the prestigious Deming Award, presented by the Union of Japanese Scientists and Engineers. For FPL the turnaround meant increased efficiency, greater financial stability, and an improved image. But the company and its customers weren't the only beneficiaries. In the process of engineering FPL's renaissance, the company's management, thanks to individuals like Dr. Wilcox, began to view manatees as assets instead of liabilities. The seasonal gathering of the endangered marine mammals at the warm-water effluents of FPL's power plants, once considered an annoyance, came to be seen as a unique public relations boon, providing an outstanding opportunity to engender a positive public attitude toward the company and its environmental efforts.

With an openness unthought of in the corporate world nearly a decade ago, Dr. Wilcox discussed FPL's change in attitude toward manatees. "When many of the traditional fresh-water springs dried up in Florida, the warm-water discharges at our plants became critical winter refuges for these animals. As a result, Florida Power and Light ended up as an unwilling host. The manatees had found a man-made thermal effluent that served their purposes, and Florida Power and Light found themselves caretakers of some of the world's most endangered mammals. But instead of treating the manatees as a liability, we decided to do more on their behalf and accept credit for our efforts."

The initial result of FPL's efforts was the distribution of a series of free educational booklets on the wildlife of Florida, including manatees. Almost a million of these have been printed to date. The public awareness program eventually expanded to include workshops, focusing on manatee biology and ecology, and the distribution of films and bumper stickers urging protection of endangered species. The company also contributes to manatee research and conservation efforts including aerial surveys, federal studies of manatee habitat, radio tracking, and the cataloging of scarred individuals. To date, the save the manatee program has cost the company an estimated eight-hundred thousand dollars.

As FPL's chief ecologist, Dr. Wilcox is responsible for overseeing the monitoring of biological systems on the company's holdings, promoting the educational programs, and acting as public relations liaison with schools, organizations, the press, and FPL employees who require information. It's a daunting task, but one that Dr. Wilcox tackles with characteristic aplomb. "As my career has developed, I'm spending less time out in the field," he noted. "I generally leave the monitoring of biological systems around our plants to consultants. I've got to rely on them. My principal function is to familiarize the public with the company's goals and its efforts to blend comfortably with the existing environment."

In many ways, Dr. Wilcox walks a fine line working as an advocate for both the power company and for manatees. He has to prove to an ever-suspicious public that a utility the size of FPL is really concerned about environmental issues, while clearly demonstrating to management that the expense involved in providing educational programs and a safe environment for manatees is worth it on the bottom line. Not that FPL didn't know that already. Back in 1974, prior to Dr. Wilcox joining the company, the Environmental Protection Agency, concerned that the warm-water discharge from the Fort Myers plant would damage the Orange River ecosystem, ordered FPL to construct cooling towers instead. When the company discovered that the manatees needed the discharge for winter habitat, the EPA rescinded its order, saving FPL an estimated 14 million dollars in construction costs.

"It doesn't take a review of the public opinion polls to know that people are very concerned about the environment and especially about manatees," explained Dr. Wilcox. "We get a lot of feedback from people who say that they're happy to have the company involved, including conservation groups who call to say that they're delighted with what we're doing. At the same time we're able to point out to management that we've been able to save the company money, avoid litigation, and help Florida Power and Light compete in today's regulatory environment. It works both ways."

Not that everything always operates smoothly. Balancing the financial concerns of company management with the environmental concerns of the regulatory agencies and the needs of the public and the manatees is a tricky business at best. One incident that clearly demonstrates the catch-22 nature of FPL's position occurred during the Christmas freeze of 1989, when sub-freezing temperatures gripped the state for an extended period of time. To escape the cold, numerous manatees headed for the warm-water effluents at FPL's power plants only to find that the water there wasn't quite warm enough. As a result, several animals died—twenty-seven in the area surrounding an FPL power plant and an adjoining Orlando utilities plant on the Indian River alone. Although the effluents from these plants are usually plenty warm enough to accommodate the needs of the manatees, the air temperatures during the freeze were so severe that the ambient water temperatures outside of the discharge area were lower than usual. The problem occurred as the result of a combination of severely cold temperatures and what the industry refers to as the Delta T factor—the 10-degree difference in temperature between the water taken in and the water discharged. Because air temperatures had dropped so low during the freeze, the ambient water temperature was cooler than usual and the Delta T factor was not warm enough to heat the ambient waters to a temperature safe enough for manatees. As a result, several animals died. Conservationists charge that since FPL has created a dependency situation, they should be responsible for ensuring that proper water temperatures are maintained, regardless of the weather.

"If you start with an ambient water temperature of seventy degrees and add the ten-degree temperature rise, then discharge is eighty degrees," Dr. Wilcox explained. "But if you start with an ambient water temperature of fifty-five degrees, then final discharge is only sixty-five degrees. Under certain circumstances, such as in the Brevard County area, animals came in looking for the thermal discharge, but it wasn't warm enough, and they were caught. The Delta T can go only so high."

The presence of FPL plants, while offering additional winter refuges, have also prevented scores of manatees from following their traditional routes south to warmer waters. This unique dependency situation could have disastrous effects on an already depleted population should Florida experience a particularly severe winter. Manatees have imprinted the location of these warm-water effluents on their traditional migratory routes. They don't know or care whether they're natural or man-made. All they're looking for is warmth. When they arrive and the water is too cold to survive, it's often too late to find another refuge.

"It's a real problem," stated Dr Wilcox. "The company is going to have to spend some money trying to solve the situation. One of the things we're thinking about is designing a manatee 'spa' of sorts where we can enclose an area near the discharge where the warm water pools and is not diluted by ambient waters. But to do something like this means you have to do some dredging and filling. And if you have to do some dredging and filling in aquatic habitat, you get involved with the strict regulations of the Environmental Protection Agency. So it's a double-edged sword."

FPL also ran into trouble in the spring and summer of 1990 when six manatees came into an intake canal at their Port Everglades power plant and either refused to leave or couldn't escape, depending on who's telling the story. For years the company operated a sea-life viewing area there, where up to five-hundred thousand visitors per year came to feed fish and view the occasional visits of manatees. In April, a mother and her calf lingered too long in the canal, gorging on handouts of junk food from the tourists.

Wildlife officials, worried that the animals refused to leave because of the handouts of food, discouraged the feeding and later urged FPL officials to close the viewing area, which they did in May. Still the mother and calf stayed. In June, they were joined by four other manatees. State and federal wildlife experts were convinced the animals were trapped, unable to swim out against the current flowing through the four 260-foot long culverts. FPL officials disagreed, noting that manatees have come and gone from their secluded intake canal since the plant began operation thirty years ago. Nevertheless, a massive rescue operation was mounted, and all six animals were captured in July. Two were released into the wild immediately. The other four, suffering from malnutrition and dehydration, were taken to Sea World and the Miami Seaquarium for rehabilitation and were later released. As a result of the incident, the U.S. Fish & Wildlife Service wants FPL to install grates across the opening of the four underwater pipes, a solution which the power company says could cost its customers from 2 to 10 million dollars. And even after the installation, debris clogging the grates could stop water flow and force a plant shutdown, according to company officials. FPL suggested trying to develop an underwater acoustical device designed to repel the animals or lure them back through the culverts should they swim into the canal. Wildlife experts believe that too little is known about the reactions of manatees to sounds to produce an acoustical device that would work with certainty. The Wildlife Service wants the grates installed.

"The wildlife agencies see it as an entrapment problem," noted Dr. Wilcox. "But we've documented since November [1990] the comings and goings of five animals in the canal. What we did was reduce the flow of water by turning off some of the pumps that bring in the water for the cooling system, allowing the manatees to swim back out through the culverts. Although installing grates would keep the animals out, it would also cause all sorts of biological fouling, corrosion, and increase the potential for clogging which would suck the canal dry and shut the plant down. It isn't as easy as it seems. Under the circumstances, we'd prefer to simply reduce flow to let the animals swim out."

To deal with such complicated situations requires not only knowledge of biological systems but also a certain political acumen, both of which Dr. Wilcox calls on daily. A native of Michigan, he came to Florida in the 1970s with a Ph.D. in Oceanography and a desire to leave his northern home for the warmer climate of the south. For the first several years he worked with The Harbor Branch Foundation, a research organization in Fort Pierce run by Seward Johnson of the Johnson & Johnson Pharmaceutical family, operating underwater research submersibles. He joined FPL in 1975 as their first ecologist at a time when the company was embroiled in a plethora of environmental problems, not the least of which was ensuring appropriate manatee habitat around its power plants. Dr. Wilcox has since played an integral role in shaping both the company's responsible environmental attitude and the public's perception of FPL as a corporate giant caring for Florida's natural giants. He is part of an eight-member Manatee Recovery Team appointed by the U.S. Fish & Wildlife Service, which represents private and public industry, conservation groups, and federal and state governments. The group meets on a periodic basis to discuss issues and develop plans to save the manatee from the brink of extinction.

One of the hazards of working for a power company the size of FPL is that you're never far from controversy, as I saw clearly demonstrated that evening at his Manatee Workshop, held at the Palm Beach Garden Community High School.

I helped him and an assistant unload boxes of manatee booklets, manatee bones for display, a projector, and loads of other paraphernalia designed to familiarize the workshop participants with manatees and their habitat. After taking a few moments to do an interview with a local television station, Dr. Wilcox strolled to the front of the auditorium to begin his presentation to the sixty or so people who sat scattered throughout the hall. The audience consisted of high school students, who were probably assigned to attend the lecture as part of classwork; local homeowners; a couple of activists, who hissed under their breath at practically everything Dr. Wilcox said; and at least one, if not two, representatives of the Marine Industries Association, a powerful special interest group representing thousands of small marine industries throughout the state that are not known for their unyielding support of manatee protection issues.

After introducing himself and showing a short film on manatees, Dr. Wilcox fielded questions from the audience before beginning a slide presentation. One of the questions focused on what was being done locally to protect manatees in the local waters.

"There's a debate going on right now about no entry and speed limit zones," he answered. "There are pros and cons to both questions. I think the governor and his cabinet will be talking about speed zone limits soon. We have seminars like this to help people understand what's involved."

After pausing for a moment, he continued. "There's also a lot of debate about propeller guards. The majority of boat kills are from large boats—cigarette boats, cruisers, the inboards. Putting propeller guards on these craft will decrease the efficiency of the motors and will cost extra. But there is technology that can be used. Tugboats have propellers six to eight feet in diameter. They use guards over these props that actually increase the efficiency of the prop by channeling water over it.

"I am a boater," he confessed, assuring the crowd that he wasn't against the recreation. "I take my eighteen- and fourteen-year-olds hypersliding. But I refuse to hyperslide in the channel where it can stir up sediment, which blocks sunlight and damages the sea grasses. We do our boating in deeper waters up in Hobe Sound. Keep in mind that the goal is not only to protect manatees but to protect their habitat as well."

Dr. Wilcox's comments stirred the Marine Industries Association representative and his colleague to action. One of the men raised his hand, stood, and asked, "What is Florida Power and Light doing for us, the taxpayers, the citizens, to protect manatees, since you caused most of this problem by having these warm-water effluents?"

Without missing a beat, Dr. Wilcox replied. "Why don't you identify yourself so the audience can know where you're coming from?"

"I'm nobody," the man replied. "I'm just an interested person."

"I believe you're with the Marine Industries Association."

"No, sir. I'm not."

By now the audience was shifting uncomfortably in their seats, not sure what all this was leading to.

"You're not?" queried Dr. Wilcox, his tone assured. "What about the person next to you?"

"My friend may be," the man admitted, somewhat hesitantly, "but I'm not."

Dr. Wilcox's tone grew flat, his delivery quick. He had obviously faced such confrontations before. "Here we go into controversy," he said, pointing at the questioner, who by now began to fidget like a perpetrator unmasked. "We've got the Marine Industries Association asking questions." Dr. Wilcox faced the crowd and addressed them directly. "As a responsibility to run the lights and the air conditioner here tonight, we have to run power plants. To meet your electrical demands. We have to run power plants that create warm water. We have federal regulations and laws that we live by. One of those regulations is called the National Pollution Discharge Elimination System Permit. It's issued by the EPA, and it regulates how we discharge our warm water. It is issued every five years and says what we can and cannot do. There's another factor that enters into this. The Endangered Species Act says that a federal agency, such as the EPA, cannot take an action that will jeopardize the continued existence of an endangered species. And a federal action is the issuance of the discharge permit. So what that means is that the EPA cannot issue a permit if it endangers the manatee. Manatees are attracted to our warm-water discharge, so the company is obligated to ensure that its activities are compatible with the well-being of the manatee. That's one of the reasons I work for the company and one of the reasons why we hold these workshops. It's that simple. We have public awareness programs, we sponsor aerial surveys, and we assist in the radio tracking of manatees."

The questioner persisted. "Other than those three things which you've been doing for years, what has Florida Power and Light got planned for the future to protect manatees?"

"Basically status quo," answered Dr. Wilcox. "Keeping our plants running, maintaining thermal discharges, looking out for the well-being of the animal, and being interactive with the state in some of their programs. Ladies and gentlemen," he added, his patience starting to ebb, "he's looking for something. But I'm not sure quite what."

"I'm not looking for anything," countered the questioner. "I just can't understand why in this time and era in our great country that a corporation as large as Florida Power and Light doesn't have something more that they're working on to save manatees?"

Wilcox responded, "The company has shown its commitment over the years through my work as a professional, as a biologist, and through its support of the activities I've already mentioned. And that's as far as the company can go."

The questioner, sensing the growing irritation of the crowd, finally sat down, his efforts to portray FPL as a villain squelched for the time being. But it's doubtful that that will be the last time that Dr. Wilcox will have to defend the activities of FPL. There are many problems to be faced in the future as manatee habitat shrinks and the power company's warm-water discharges become even more critical to the survival of this endangered species. One of these issues concerns the inevitablity of closing down old facilities. According to Dr. Wilcox, the answer lies in repowering the old units for new generation, a process which would ensure the continuance of a warm-water discharge for generations to come, maintaining the integrity of a critical manatee habitat.

As I watched him pack up his equipment, the crowd long since dispersed, I realized that the process of changing attitudes is a long and tedious task requiring unerring patience and persistence. Trying to be a watchdog for an endangered species from inside a company that is viewed alternately as a great savior or part of the problem must be a lot like being a double agent in a spy thriller. No one is ever really sure what side you're on, but the mission is always clear to you.

I decided to seek a broad perspective on the issue from Judith Delaney Vallee, executive director of the Save the Manatee Club (SMC), and one of the key voices in Florida's growing environmental movement. I visited her at her office in Maitland, Florida, to ask how she viewed FPL's role in saving the manatee.

"I think they're a mixed bag and a blessing," she answered with characteristic frankness. "Historically, the winter range of mana-tees was much more southerly. The power plants have sort of lured them away from their traditional migration, although in truth there wasn't much luring to be done, because there was no place else for them to go other than a few natural springs. The power plants have offered additional habitat, but they've also introduced new prob-lems, like the Delta T issue. The power companies know they are responsible for these manatees. I think they're prepared to live up to that responsibility, although once capital outlay to protect manatees starts to involve millions of dollars to fix up plants and so forth, it's hard to say."

"Have their public awareness programs helped your group gain support?" I asked, pointing to a couple of FPL manatee booklets in her office.

"Their programs are wonderful, and they distribute excellent literature, not only for manatees but for sea turtles, panthers, alligators, and wood storks. They're first-rate education-wise, and there's no doubt their efforts have increased public awareness. But we may find out down the road that the power companies represent a catch twenty-two situation. For example, we know that the few remaining Florida panthers are getting mercury in their system. We think it's from the fish they eat. And we think the power plants are part of the mercury discharge. We believe that water and air pollution and chemicals from herbicides and pesticides used throughout the state are wreaking havoc on wildlife in Florida, but we have little scientific data to support the charge. Should we find out down the road that the power plants are part of this, we could end up in a difficult situation. On the one hand we need the power plants for electricity and for critical manatee habitat, but what if they're part of the problem?"

Sitting in Judith's office surrounded by posters, pamphlets, piles of legislative documents, and scores of phone messages, I felt as if I had my finger on the pulse of manatee activism. The offices of the SMC are located on the second floor of a nondescript three-story white stucco building about fifteen minutes from Orlando. Its unassuming location belies the Club's remarkable growth as an effective educational and lobbying force. Established in 1981 by former Florida Governor Bob Graham and singer/songwriter Jimmy Buffett, the Club has grown into a powerful national nonprofit organization with over twenty-seven thousand members representing every state and many foreign countries.

At first growth came slow. The club started as a public awareness organization, sending speakers and educational materials to community groups and public schools, picking up members here and there. After a couple of years, membership was still counted in the hundreds. Then in November 1984, the SMC kicked off the Adopt-A-Manatee program, where for fifteen dollars members could choose a manatee for "adoption" and receive a description and photo of "their" manatee. By the time Judith came on board four months later, membership had grown to over three thousand. Now it's close to ten times that number.

"We, and by 'we' I mean the collective membership, are extremely influential because we're involved early in the process of manatee protection," noted Judith proudly. "Even before a rule is written on local protection plans, we ask our members to write and get involved earlier and earlier in the process of decision making. So rather than taking a reactive position on issues, we're taking a proactive position. And it works."

SMC recommendations have been incorporated into numerous rules throughout the state designed to protect manatees, many of them due to active letter-writing campaigns and work by SMC biologists and staff members. At a time when legislators consider twenty-five letters on an issue a "landslide issue," receiving hundreds of letters on manatee issues make them truly stand up and take notice. Although the concept is simple, the task of being the environmental watchdog for the phenomenal growth of coastal Florida is grueling and unrelenting. In one area, members are urged to attend legislative sessions in Tallahassee, while members in another area are asked to write letters to the U.S. Fish & Wildlife Service to complain about a city's noncompliance with manatee protection laws at their municipal marina. Florida is a big state, and there are laws and permits being reviewed almost every day that have a direct or indirect effect on the survival of manatees. And many of the assaults on manatees and their habitat come from unexpected sources that can surprise even the most vigilant organizations.

One example of this occurred in late 1990 when the Club learned from one of its members that the Offshore Professional Tour planned to race some of the world's largest powerboats in Hillsborough Bay, near Tampa, at the same time that manatees begin to congregate there for the winter. The race and the thousands of boats that would gather there to watch the event could spell disaster for the ninety or so manatees that move into the area seasonally.

"What happened in this case is representative of how poorly manned the Fish and Wildlife Service is and how stressed the few people are that they have reviewing permits," noted Judith. "When the Fish and Wildlife staff went to review the boat race permit, they neglected to use the DNR database, which clearly shows that Tampa Bay is an important area for manatees. So, when the Coast Guard consulted with the Wildlife Service under Section Six of the Endangered Species Act, the Service, not having the up-to-date data, said Tampa Bay is not an area of really great concern for the manatee."

After the Coast Guard issued the permit, a concerned citizen alerted the Club, which quickly sprang into action. They arranged a meeting with the DNR, the Coast Guard, and race officials and had their legal counsel begin preparing an emergency speed zone rule that would have excluded the race from the Bay. But before any legal action took place, the Wildlife Service bowed to the public outcry and rescinded the race permit.

As a result of the incident, the Club and the Florida Audubon Society petitioned Florida's governor and cabinet to adopt a rule amendment requiring individuals or organizations holding motor-boat races over state-owned water bottoms, called Sovereign Submerged Lands, to obtain short-term leases. The rule prohibited powerboat races on any bay or estuary in the state or in the vicinity of coral reef formations, especially over state-owned submerged lands where manatees were at risk. Ironically, the Club found out that the state doesn't own the bottom lands in Tampa Bay—it had deeded the submerged lands there to the Tampa Port Authority. If their rule had been adopted, it would not have affected Tampa Bay after all.

Judith's first taste of manatee activism was much less successful but was critical to her future career. She left her home in the Bronx, New York, in 1977 to do some extensive world traveling in search of an alternative lifestyle, which to that point had involved studying art history in college and working as a secretary at *Scholastic* magazine. She ended up renting an apartment on a waterway in Fort Lauderdale. On the second day there she strolled out onto a dock behind her home and saw several manatees surface nearby with a boat in hot pursuit. Incensed, she went inside and called the Marine Patrol to complain. They told her there was nothing they could do. "You haven't heard the last of me," she stammered with more than a little prescience.

She laughed as she recalled the story. "I don't think I've ever been more angry about anything else. I 'shot from the hip' and circulated a neighborhood petition proposing to turn the waterway into a manatee sanctuary. I was naive but determined. The matter did come before the boating advisory council in Fort Lauderdale, and we were able to get a good number of people down there for the hearing. When our agenda item finally came up, the council chairman said, 'You don't need a manatee sanctuary with regulated speed zones. Just go outside, stand on your dock, and throw tomatoes at speeding boaters.' That was his advice," she said with obvious disgust. "And it represented many people's attitudes in government back then."

Despite the initial failure, Judith had found a cause, and she pursued it with a vengeance. She volunteered her time with the

Broward County Audubon Society for a year and a half before hearing of the opening at the SMC. Now government officials are careful about what sort of inane advice they give to Judith or any of the Club members.

"When I was a volunteer, no one ever wanted to take the time to talk with me," she recalled with a wry smile. "Now we pick up the phone and spend a great deal of time talking with agencies, politicians, and other officials trying to influence more positive action on behalf of the manatees and their habitat. That's one of the most rewarding things we do."

The Club also plays a key role in publicizing the plight of manatees nationally, distributing 1,600 press kits each year to newspapers, magazines, and television and radio stations around the country. Their efforts have resulted in numerous stories on manatees in such publications as *Life* magazine and on national television networks and affiliates throughout the United States.

Ironically, Judith rarely gets to see the animals she protects so fervently. The demands of the job prevent her from visiting her charges but once every sixteen months or so. "I envy someone like Wayne [Hartley] because he's out there all the time," she noted with resignation. "He's a great person who has the best job of all of us. Unfortunately, I can't enjoy seeing manatees too often. There's too much else going on."

According to Judith, the common denominator in all the problems facing manatees is human overpopulation. "A thousand new residents a day settle in Florida, and the state just can't handle it. When people ask me what's so important about manatees becoming extinct, I tell them that manatee extinction is just a symptom of the real problem, which is finite state resources under assault by the sheer number of people moving here. I think Florida, California, and Hawaii are suffering especially because they have fragile ecosystems, although Florida now has the dubious distinction of having the highest number of threatened and endangered species in the contiguous United States."

She provided some remarkable statistics. "About eighty percent of the people who come here move to the coastal zone. Everybody wants to live on the water and have a boat. We're getting about one hundred new boat registrations daily. Add that to the one million boats plying our waterways now and you can see where the additional problems come: the dredging and filling of wetlands, the destruction of sea-grass beds, which provide food and habitat for fish of all kinds as well as manatees, and nonstop coastal and marine development."

In a position where daily statistics can seem more depressing than illuminating, Judith finds magic in the cause and in the animals she fights for. "One of our lobbyists said it best," recalled Judith, pointing out one of the saddest facts. "When you think about it, the majority of manatees in the state of Florida at any given time are in the process of healing from an encounter with a boat. That, to me, is what keeps me going. Manatees don't have a chance if someone doesn't speak out. I'm cause-oriented—a Type A personality—and I personally can't stand injustice. Manatees, to me, epitomize injustice because they are victims of our progress and frivolity. We jump in our boats and are killing in very, very painful ways. So I have to do something about it."

Leaning forward in her chair, she added, "I have to be honest with you. I once tried to look the other way, at one time even thinking of moving out of state. But I just couldn't. Now I'm more hardened because when people call and ask me if some manatees swimming off their dock near boats can be moved to a safer place." She concluded with a sense of foreboding, "There is no safer place."

Is it true that people are really unwilling to change habits, that there is no safe place left for manatees? In the midst of a boating public that grows by leaps and bounds each day, the SMC found one enlightening statistic. In July and August 1989, they hired the Survey Research Laboratory, Policy Sciences Program, at Florida State University to conduct a survey of 911 registered boat owners in Florida. Ninety-one percent of the boaters polled supported programs to protect the manatee, even if it meant reducing the speed on some waterways. The same percentage supported setting speed or wake limits in areas where natural resources such as sea grasses need protecting. In short, the poll indicated extremely strong support for improved boating safety and manatee protection. As a result of the study, it seems that the boating industry, which plays a key role in foiling the efforts of conservation groups involved in manatee protection legislation, can no longer claim with validity that it represents the voice of the boating public, although David Ray, president of the state's Marine Industries Association, told me he felt the survey questions were asked in such a way as to elicit positive responses toward the save-the-manatee cause.

Despite boater attitudes for or against protective legislation, manatees will undoubtedly continue to be injured and killed by boats simply because of the sheer numbers of boaters and the slow surface behavior of the animals. When injuries occur, there are two primary facilities within the state qualified to rescue and rehabilitate injured or orphaned manatees—the Miami Seaquarium and Sea World in Orlando. A third facility at the Lowry Park Zoo in Tampa—the 3.3-million-dollar Manatee and Aquatic Center—opened in January 1990, but, unlike the facilities in Miami and Orlando, it is not yet authorized by the U.S. Fish & Wildlife Service for manatee rescues. Due to its brief history, manatee medicine and rehabilitation is still an inexact science with many frontiers left to explore, but one of the state's recognized experts is research biologist Dr. Dan Odell of Sea World, who has been mentor for many of the young biologists now working with the animals statewide.

After seeing several examples of the amazing resilience of severely injured manatees at both Crystal River and Blue Spring, I decided to pay Dr. Odell a visit to learn a little more about the practice of manatee medicine at Sea World. We met under typically blue Florida skies on a walkway in the midst of three large manatee tanks in an area that Hollywood veterans might refer to as the back lot. The animal care area sits isolated from the public exhibits. There are no crowds, refreshment stands, or grandstands, just numerous tanks full of honking, barking, squeaking and bellowing aquatic creatures, ranging from sea lions and sea turtles to dolphins and manatees. The low, steady hum of pool filtration systems serves as a constant reminder that this is a manufactured environment designed to mimic the natural world; water temperatures must be maintained, pool water must be constantly filtered and cleaned, and the backlot residents must be carefully monitored twenty-four hours a day, seven days a week. Rescue and rehabilitation facilities, like those found at Sea World, have adapted the latest technology to master the mimicry of natural environments. As we leaned against the Beached Animal Recovery Pool, two recovering manatees made their way to the side nearest us, nuzzling the pool wall and lifting their great heads to within inches of our arms. Smiling at our two curious visitors, Dr. Odell talked about some of the more common cases of manatee injuries.

"We get animals in here with severe wounds, some where propellers have literally opened up their body," he noted as he gestured toward the healing scars of one of the manatees swimming in the larger pool. "Once the body cavity has been penetrated and water goes in, it's just about all over. They may still be alive but the prognosis is poor. Other animals may have their fluke nearly or completely cut off. Sometimes we get animals with very few signs of external injuries, but they've been brought in because their behavior isn't quite normal, which gives us a clue that something is amiss.

Quite often they die shortly after they're picked up, then we find massive internal damage—ribs have been broken and are poking through the lungs or the skull is massively fractured. These are boat impact injuries, most likely from a very fast boat. Obviously we also get cases where the injuries aren't quite so severe. As long as we can get them before massive infection has set in, they have a pretty good chance of pulling through."

In the rescue of manatees, timing is everything. A well-intentioned but erroneous report of an ailing manatee can send a crew of five or six specialists scurrying to a distant site hours away only to find a content, resting manatee. Dr. Odell remembers receiving a frantic call once reporting a group of very active manatees. The caller was concerned that something was seriously wrong. After asking a few key questions, Dr. Odell assured the worried caller that everything was all right. It was a mating group. On the other hand, too much delay in responding to a call can mean death for a severely injured animal. To evaluate and carry out rescues, Dr. Odell and his colleagues rely on individuals such as Vic Aderholt, an animal care supervisor at Sea World, who heads up a team of specialists trained in marine mammal rescue procedures.

A thin but rugged individual, Vic has supervised numerous rescues of stranded marine mammals from manatees to dolphins, each of which present their own unique set of problems. Because of the size of the beached-animal recovery van—a stretch vehicle loaded with all the latest rescue equipment, ranging from closed-cell, high-density foam to custom-built stretchers and a cellular phone—each rescue can accommodate only five or six people. Each of them have to be prepared to lift weighty victims, a few of whom can exceed 2,000 pounds. Once at the rescue site, there's always the problem of capturing the animal.

Vic recalled a recent rescue as an example. "On one of our recent manatee recoveries, we arrived at a canal that was about fifty feet wide by ten feet deep. There were manatees everywhere, and the water was so murky, visibility was zero. In this giant gathering of manatees was the animal we had been called to rescue. It had several severe propeller slashes on its right side and was very lethargic. We couldn't just cast a large net over all the manatees because that would have caused mass panic. So, as we're standing there trying to figure out what to do, the injured manatee makes its way to within ten feet of the sea wall where we were standing.

"It wasn't really too active, but manatees have a curious habit of coming to life when a net hits the water, so at first we were hesitant to just throw a net and hope for good luck. But the sun was setting, and it was starting to get dark. We had no choice."

Vic and his crew lined up on the sea wall and began swinging the large heavy net rhythmically. After building up the momentum necessary to cast a 25-foot, lead-weighted net several feet, they let go on the count of three, and the huge net sailed right over the manatee, hitting the murky water with a resounding splash.

A smile creased Vic's face as he continued the story. "The manatee took a breath and disappeared. We were standing there staring, straining for any sign that we had caught her. We jumped in the water and started to pull on the net and there was nothing. We figured she had somehow gotten out. But all of a sudden we felt a yank, and there she was, right in the middle of the net."

According to Vic, manatees don't have very good eyesight at close range but have a well-developed sense of hearing and an uncanny sense of touch. "They have sensory hairs, like whiskers, all over their body, which they use to evade capture. You can put your net in the murkiest water, with muck swirling everywhere, and if there's a hole, they'll find it and get through. There's even a possibility they may use echolocation, like whales and dolphins, although no one has ever confirmed the theory."

Although it's an intriguing subject, little is known about manatee communication. While they may use such refined methods as echolocation, which is the ability to emit sound pulses and read the returning echoes to find one's way in a murky environment, or to communicate, scientists have yet to adequately determine the full range of manatees' sensory skills. They do emit squeals and squeaks within the human auditory range, usually when they are frightened, sexually aroused, playing, or swimming with calves. As a result, most scientists believe that sound, including a certain degree of ultrasonic reception, plays the key role in manatee communication.

But for Vic and the rescue team, it's usually the touch of the net that can send an animal into a panicked flurry. "If you do manage to surround one with a net," he noted with clear concern, "manatees tend to get a bit frantic and will eventually run into the net and start spinning. And that's when you can get into some pretty interesting, serious situations."

At that point, the communication of the rescue team is more important than communication of the manatee. Each man has to avoid getting entangled in the net. It doesn't take a lot of imagination to understand what could happen to an individual who gets tied up with a rolling, spinning, and thrashing 1,000- to 2,000-pound animal. Once subdued, the manatee has to be carried back to its foam bed in the van. Oftentimes the short, but laborious, journey involves walking up muddy riverbanks while holding on to the canvas stretcher and its weighty cargo for dear life. Since manatees tend to fight restraint of any kind, special precautions are taken to limit their mobility during transport. Even the custom stretchers have no holes for the pectoral fins to poke through, because manatees are capable of lifting themselves up and out of the stretcher with their flippers. Since the trip back to Sea World can be lengthy—the Sea World team covers most of the middle and northern part of the state twenty-four hours a day, each day of the year—the rescue team is able to administer medicine and routine injections under a veterinarian's direction. Once at Sea World, the animals begin a period of recuperation that can last from months to years, depending on the severity of the case. Because of the endangered status of manatees, the biologists and veterinarians at Sea World tend to be conservative in their treatment, preferring to keep an animal a little longer to ensure that all is well before releasing it back into the wild.

Treating severe injuries quickly is the key to survival for any mammal, including man. But manatee physiology offers the sort of challenges that staff veterinarians at Sea World simply can't answer with textbooks.

"I think it's fair to say that the folks that have been doing manatee rescue and rehabilitation over the past several years are really writing the book on manatee medicine," noted Dr. Odell. "Treatments are far ahead of what they were ten years ago mostly because there are a great many medical techniques that can be applied, whether it's simply X-raying, CAT scanning, thermal imaging, or using large-animal anesthesia."

Treatment of an ailing manatee involves teamwork that goes beyond the confines of Sea World. Experts from throughout the state, including specialists at the University of Florida College of Veterinary Medicine and the Miami Seaquarium, will often be consulted. It's a time-consuming, costly process with a single goal—returning the animals to their natural environment as quickly as possible.

Dr. Odell saw his first manatee, an Amazonian specimen, at the Steinhart Aquarium in San Francisco back in the late 1960s. Immediately he felt that the anatomy of these unique marine mammals, which few knew anything about, represented a "biological gold mine" just waiting to be discovered. By the time he began his work on manatees back in 1974, they were an endangered and protected species and not the sort of creatures you could capture, euthanize, then dissect to study their unique anatomy. And as any medical or veterinary student knows, much of the familiarity with animal physiology comes from the study of dead specimens. To alleviate the situation, Dr. Odell cofounded the Carcass Salvage Program with the U.S. Fish & Wildlife Service to study the natural history of manatees and, when possible, the cause of death. As he originally suspected, he had uncovered a tremendous source of biological data on a vanishing species.

"Manatees are a biological curiosity," he commented as he rubbed the grizzled snout of our curious friend, who faithfully hovered at the pool's edge as if listening to our conversation. "Their internal anatomy is so different that I was really surprised when I saw some of the organ placements. I had a number of graduate students at the time whose degrees depended upon helping out with the salvage program. Many went on to write their masters theses and doctoral dissertations on portions of manatee physiology. Essentially we went out and learned together."

Despite all that has been learned in the past few decades, Dr. Odell feels that biologists have just scratched the surface in their study of the manatee. Although their physical similarities to whales and dolphins carry over to certain aspects of their general adaptation to the marine environment, such as diving and respiratory physiology, little else is known about a manatee's physical and behavioral makeup. Do they need to drink fresh water? If so, how long can they go without it? What is the physiological nature of their response to cold weather? How good is their fat as insulation? Using noninvasive techniques developed to study other marine mammals such as cetaceans, sea lions, and sea otters, research biologists like Dr. Odell hope to uncover many of the secrets that could help to sustain manatees in the wild.

"You can learn just as much from a live manatee as you can from a dead manatee in terms of quantity," he noted, commenting on the use of noninvasive and invasive techniques. "But both methods of study complement each other, much like laboratory and field studies. What we learn with captive animals helps observers in the field, and what they see out there with free-ranging animals helps us interpret what we see here."

Besides his long-time work with manatees, Dr. Odell is also a founder and the scientific coordinator of the Southeastern U.S. Marine Mammal Stranding Network, a nationwide network of marine scientists, biologists, and universities who research beached and stranded marine mammals in order to prevent catastrophic marine diseases and deaths caused by human interaction. In April 1990, he was personally presented with a "Point of Light" award by President George Bush for his efforts relating to the Stranding Network.

Working with both whales and manatees provides Dr. Odell with a rare perspective on two very different types of animals facing very similar problems, although he feels that manatees have yet to capture the extensive attention afforded cetaceans.

"I don't think the problems facing manatees receive the same level of public attention as the whale issue simply because their distribution is so limited," he pointed out. "They also don't have the 'glamour' of fast-moving whales and dolphins, although the level of awareness has increased dramatically through the efforts of a lot of different organizations like Sea World, the DNR, Florida Power and Light, and the Save the Manatee Club. Still, you'll find people out there, even in this state, who don't know what manatees are or what they look like."

To illustrate his point, Dr. Odell provided a few examples. "I was on a hike once with Boy Scouts along the edge of Biscayne Bay in Miami, and we were talking about manatees. They were all saying

'We've never seen a manatee out there.' I looked up, pointed, and said, 'What's that? There's one now!' They couldn't believe their eyes!

"Another time I was on a pier talking to a fisherman who told me he had fished the same spot for twenty years and had never seen a manatee. At that moment I looked down and there was one swimming right under our noses."

He laughed. "Awareness is up, but we're not done yet. We have to keep at it."

Although he doesn't usually accompany rescue trips, Dr. Odell, whose automobile license plate reads SEACOW 2 (SEACOW 1 was stolen in Miami), can recall his share of humorous incidents relating to the rescue program. He told me of a particularly curious incident involving two adults, a child, and what must have been a decomposing manatee.

An adult who had sighted a floating carcass called the salvage team to report a dead manatee. The Florida Marine Patrol, which usually responds to calls first to confirm sightings, towed the animal to the nearest boat ramp for an inspection. Both adults were convinced it was a manatee.

"No, that's not a manatee," said a child standing nearby, who had obviously studied manatees in school. "It's a shark."

The adults, however, weren't convinced. The Marine Patrol officer checked it again. "Yes," he confirmed. "That's a manatee."

Insistent but respectful, the boy said, "No, it's a shark."

Ignoring the boy's comments, the officer called in the salvage team, who arrived onsite shortly afterward. Sure enough, it was a dead shark.

"I've had things like that happen to me a lot," laughed Dr. Odell, who was careful to compliment the Marine Patrol, noting that they are an integral part of the rescue team efforts. "We've gone after dead hogs, washed up jewfish. All sorts of things."

Despite the light moments, the salvage team and the bevy of veterinarians and biologists at Sea World take their jobs very seriously and are committed to changing the course of events for manatees. Dr. Odell believes that education is the key and hopes to have a manatee education area someday at Sea World with a large display of manatee models and skeletons perhaps even a public exhibit with a few live manatees to expose the greater public to the plight of a highly endangered animal.

Like Judith and Wayne, Dr. Odell views the manatee issue as a symptom of a larger environmental problem. "People and their boating activities are the primary cause of problems for manatees and the natural habitat. And these activities also affect sea-grass beds," he added. "If we can slow boats down, that means fewer injuries to manatees, less wake, less turbidity, and less erosion of the sea-grass beds, which are not only critical for manatees but for many species out there like fish, shrimp, and ultimately, man."

Sea grasses are submerged, flowering plants commonly found in estuaries where salt and fresh water mix. Of the fifty-two species of sea grasses worldwide, seven are found in protected bays and lagoons around Florida, which feature the right amount of light, shallow depth, and the clear water necessary for the grasses to thrive. Sea-grass beds are some of the most productive communities on Earth, providing vital nursery areas for a remarkable variety of marine life, including fish, crustaceans, and shellfish. They also perform other vital functions such as ensuring clear water by trapping sediments on their leaves and helping to prevent bottom erosion—much like grass on a hillside prevents soil erosion. Today, sea-grass beds throughout Florida, like the manatees, are also under siege from rapid coastal development, water pollution, slashing boat propellers, and boat wake turbidity—all of which contribute to increased sediment build up that blocks the sunlight so vital to a thriving sea-grass bed. As sea grasses throughout the state die, there are fewer beds available to stem the growing storm of sediment, resulting in reduced water quality and visibility—the beginning-of-the-end cycle for Florida's famed waters and the food and sport they provide. If water quality continues to decay, replanting of sea-grass beds is not an option, as sediments will prevent healthy growth. And the problem is already severe. Tampa Bay, for instance, has lost 81 percent of its sea-grass beds.

The plight of the manatee is as much a story of the survival of the Florida ecosystem as it is of the battle to save a single species. For the individuals who keep watch on the dissolution of a fragile environment, the urgency grows daily, the task becomes ever greater and more imposing. But they, like scores of other marine scientists and committed conservationists, maintain a clear vision, a certain hope, that transcends the gloom of reality, illuminating a path for a future where answers will be found.

A SHRINKING WORLD

We reach backward to our parents and forward to our children and through their children to a future we will never see, but about which we need to care.
—Carl Jung

Looking down on the Florida landscape during a mid-winter flight, I gazed at the neat geometric patterns formed by man's encroachment far below. Each tiny circle, each wedge-shaped slice, delineated real estate developments from the orange groves, pastures from municipalities. Ponds, lakes, sinkholes, and swamps were sprinkled among the greenery, each a golden reflective mirror in the early morning sunlight, as our plane passed over their watery expanse.

From 5 miles up, the world looks decidedly smaller, its resources visibly finite. Rivers snake like life-giving arteries through the countryside, their wild meanderings unimaginably chaotic: thin ribbons of fragile fluid branching off into tributaries and minor streams stretching to the horizon. Cities too large to take in from street level lose all vertical dimension and appear white and pockmarked, in stark contrast to the smooth, dark green and brown colors of the outlying countryside.

In the few short decades since I first visited Florida, the perspective from the air has changed dramatically. The wide open spaces have been divided and subdivided into mile after mile of housing tracts and commercial developments. The unspoiled look of the countryside has been altered to conform to the comforts of late twentieth-century civilization: neatly paved roads, fast food/gas store on every corner, and acre after acre of asphalt parking lots and strip malls. To accommodate all this growth, Florida is selling its soul to developers, and it's costing dearly. Roughly 411 acres of the state's forests disappear each day, and only 350 miles of the 1,197 miles of Florida beaches remain undeveloped. As a result, Florida's unique wildlife and fragile ecosystem have taken a backseat to the pursuit of the good life. Florida is a state under siege. And no where is it more evident than from the air.

Retirees continue to flock to the state to enjoy the advantages of warm sun and low taxes. Political refugees from the Caribbean basin chase their dreams of freedom on its sandy soil. And the young and upwardly mobile choose its growing affluence to enhance their lifestyles. In all, over a thousand people a day move to its sandy shores, one of the highest growth rates in the nation for a state that already ranks fourth in population nationally. Add to that the 39 million visitors a year who enjoy the magic of its remarkable recreational facilities, and you've got the makings of a potential ecological disaster. Too many people, too little space. In Florida, as in many other areas of the world, overpopulation is nearing a crisis with dire consequences for the quality of air, water, wetlands, beaches, and other natural resources.

In the years since the outspoken activism of the 1960s, the issue of uncontrolled population growth has diminished from a flame to a minor spark, barely turning the head of the average consumer of the 1990s. Back then there were national demonstrations, international conferences, even best-selling books—all focused on zero population growth as an integral part of saving our planet. But as we traversed the intervening decades, our thoughts and concerns changed from a global perspective to an inward focus. The "Me Generation" became part of our vocabulary, and materialism reigned supreme. Activists grew older, perhaps a little tired, and the younger generation simply knew no better or didn't seem to care. In the interim, the problem of a burgeoning world population never disappeared, it simply became more acute. And it's not just a Third World problem.

Dr. Paul Ehrlich, Bing Professor of Population Studies at Stanford University and coauthor of the 1968 bestseller, *The Population Bomb*, argues in his new book, *The Population Explosion*, that "arresting global population growth should be second in importance only to avoiding nuclear war." And he offers some convincing arguments to support his point. In the twenty-four years since he wrote his bestseller, 1.8 billion people have been added to the world's population, with 95 million people joining the crowd each year. To put this in perspective, he estimates that it took roughly 4 million years for the world to attain a population of 2 billion people at the time of his birth in 1932. Since then, in roughly sixty years, we've added 3.3 billion more people. By the turn of the century, the world will be struggling to accommodate over 6 billion people, a staggering number of humans when you take into account the need to supply food and water from an environment already reeling from abuse. Overpopulation has to do with not only numbers of people; but also with their impact on the earth's life-support systems.

According to Dr. Ehrlich, the United States, as the world's fourth largest nation, probably has the world's worst population problem because we live in a society based on planned obsolescence. Everything is thrown away: an inefficient and wasteful lifestyle based on environmentally destructive technologies and conspicuous consumption. As a result, Dr. Ehrlich notes, ecologically the birth of an American baby represents "Twenty to one hundred times the disaster for the planet's life-support systems as the birth of a baby in Bangladesh or Kenya or India." The explosive growth in these poorer countries, while still a major cause of global environmental deterioration, does not impact the environment as much as excessive population growth in wealthy countries where affluence increases consumption and hence, waste.

In Florida, affluence means a home on the coast, plenty of opportunities for outdoor recreation, and a boat. In many instances, this spells disaster for manatees. With over a million boats so far, an additional three-hundred thousand that visit the state's waters, and over a hundred new boat registrations daily, Florida is the nation's fastest growing recreational boating state. By the year 2000, there will be over 1.6 million vessels using 8,426 miles of salt-water tidal coastline, 2 million acres of natural lakes, 1 million acres of man-made lakes, and 11,909 miles of rivers and streams. The telling part of these statistics is the fact that while boat registrations climb, available waters will increase barely, if at all. As a result, the waters of Florida will become an increasingly hostile environment for the animal treasured as the state's official marine mammal—the manatee.

As of now, collisions with boats and barges account for approximately one in every four manatee deaths, with 1989 and 1991 recording the two highest yearly totals—fifty-one and fifty-three, respectively—since manatee mortality statistics were first compiled by the Florida DNR in 1974. In those years, 484 manatee deaths have been directly attributed to collisions with watercraft, far exceeding any other known cause of death. In light of these numbers, the recreational boating industry has been fingered as the primary threat to the survival of the manatee, a charge that boating industry representatives consider unfair.

John Lowe, a Jacksonville marine industry lobbyist and former president of the Marine Industries Association, an organization representing approximately 1,500 boating-related industries throughout the state, has been involved with the manatee issue both as a representative of the Association and as a member of the

U.S. Fish & Wildlife Manatee Recovery Team. He feels the focus of responsibility should be shifted from the number of boats to the training of boat owners. "Manatees are a people problem," he stated emphatically, "not just a boat problem. I think education is the key. Everyone should know what a manatee is and what to look for at the surface when you're in manatee territory."

As proof of his commitment to the issue, he pointed out that he helped sponsor the Mandatory Violator Education Program through the state legislature several years ago. As a result, individuals ticketed for boating violations are required to attend safety courses, a portion of which focus on the identification of manatees. He bristled at the suggestion that more boat speed regulations and protected aquatic habitats are needed to prevent the extinction of the manatee. "Those who are concerned about saving manatees are trying to burden taxpayers with too much regulation," he noted. "I agree that if there's one manatee who dies from abuse, that's too many. We want to protect the species, but not to the extent that the protection kills a 3.5 billion dollar boating industry and all the employees who count on its survival."

Boating *is* big business in Florida. The 3.5-billion-dollar figure Lowe mentioned represents monies spent *yearly* on boating-related industries, ranking it right up there with tourism as one of Florida's leading industries. In 1989, boat sales in Florida reached 854,217,000 dollars—tops in the nation. If you consider the 42,000 Floridians employed by the industry and the 72 million dollars in annual sales taxes it represents, you get the idea that marine industries have some financial and political clout. But environmentalists have made great strides in building public support for their cause by casting special interest groups like the Marine Industries Association in an adversarial role, a position that David Ray, current president of the Association, feels is unwarranted.

"We're not anti-manatee," he stated emphatically. "Boaters are conservationists too. Water isn't pleasant if it isn't clean and if the manatee and its habitat isn't properly preserved. But there's got to be a balance. People have a right to decide how much they're going to give up to save whatever it is they want to save. And that's where the balance of giving needs to come—from the users and the environmentalists."

Lowe agrees. "Overregulation is the problem," he noted. "Instead of a few regulations designed to regulate boating activities, they want to bury us with regulations aimed at protecting manatees."

"I think the marine industries are afraid people are going to stop buying boats," countered Judith Vallee. "They don't want the government telling them what to do. A lot of people call the nation's waterways the 'last frontier' where you can do whatever you want. But that's absolutely got to change if manatees are to survive in Florida."

The clash between manatee advocates and the boating industry involves numerous issues, including more regulated speed zones, licenses for boat operators, and additional manatee sanctuaries—all of which manatee experts generally agree are necessary to protect both manatees and the state's fragile marine ecosystem. Marine industry interests, however, take a different view.

The Florida DNR recently recommended that statewide speed limits be established for boats, not only to provide additional protection for manatees, but to enhance protection for the state's natural resources. High boating speeds contribute to manatee mortality as well as the human fatality rate, which in Florida is twice the national average. The DNR also believes that boating licenses should be issued to the 4 million or more people who operate vessels on the state's waterways, with a portion of the licensing fee appropriated to enhance boating safety and law enforcement capabilities. Although boat operators are required to abide by existing boating laws, there is currently no requirement for them to become familiar with them: a system that punishes incompetency but does nothing to discourage it. And with only 235 Marine Patrol officers statewide to enforce boating laws and to watch over twenty-two manatee protection zones stretched across thousands of miles of coastline, enforcement, or the lack of it, is an issue that plays an integral role in the fate of manatees.

Perhaps the most critical concern for manatee advocates is the establishment of zones to provide manatees and sea grasses protection from the damage incurred from slashing boat propellers. Shoreland buffer zones and no-entry zones for boats are under consideration throughout the state, but have met considerable opposition from marine industry lobbyists and commercial and sports fishermen.

Ray voiced one of the key objections to the protection zones. "One of the waterways in this state is just about to be closed to boaters during the winter, except for the people who live up there," he noted with some aggravation. "The reasoning is purportedly based on scientific evidence that they've seen manatees nursing, calving, and mating in these waters. Even if this is true, no one's ever done a study to see if a boat idling by almost motionless will cause a manatee not to reproduce or calve. If a boat's going very slow, manatees just go about their business."

Ray's point may be viable, but he's assuming one thing that may not always be a constant: a slow boat. If indeed manatees are unaffected by idling boats, there is plenty of physical evidence to show that they are also injured severely by careless boaters. To keep the waterway open to all vessels would be to assume that everyone will act responsibly while passing through the area, and perhaps that's assuming too much, considering the statistics.

The DNR views the licensing of boat operators as one way to ensure boating responsibility. But the Marine Industries Association sees licenses as nothing more than a hidden tax. "We're opposed to licensing boat operators, because there's no education involved," stated Ray. "It's just like taking a test for a driver's license. You study for fifteen minutes, take a test, walk out, and forget the whole thing. That doesn't make you a better driver.

"We believe that a good boating course is what's needed, with a certificate issued like there is for the U.S. Power Squadron or Coast Guard Auxiliary boating safety courses. Then there's no bureacracy involved."

The DNR's proposal does involve some education, specifically for individuals twelve years of age or above who want to operate a boat, but who are not licensed to drive an automobile. They would be required to complete a boater education course. The other advantage to the proposal is the enforcement aspect. A point system for violations would be established, similar to the existing system for motor vehicle offenders, allowing the state to suspend or revoke boating privileges for serious or repeat offenders.

Another regulator consideration looming over Florida's heated environmental politics is one that could make a dramatic impact on additional coastal development—protection of state-owned submerged bottom lands. Sovereignty submerged lands, as defined by the state, include "tidal lands, islands, sand bars, shallow banks, and lands waterward of the ordinary or mean high water line, under navigable fresh and salt waters." Florida's Internal Improvement Trust Fund Board of Trustees is responsible for overseeing the administration, management, and disposition of sovereignty lands. Any activity that involves use of these lands, such as the construction of docks, piers, boat ramps, mooring pilings, or any dredging, has to be approved by the board, which then issues a consent for land use, a lease, an easement, or approves an outright sale of the bottom land. According to the state's Sovereignty Submerged Lands Management plan, such activities have to be designed "to minimize or eliminate adverse impacts on fish and wildlife habitat," with special consideration "given to endangered and threatened species habitat."

With development running rampant throughout the state, there is little doubt that much of Florida's ecological system is being adversely impacted by the increased contruction along its coasts, including the building of new marinas to accommodate the growing number of boats. But in October 1990, when the state passed a controversial rule limiting boat slips to one per 100 feet of shoreline, marine industry lobbyists were shocked. One lobbyist, quoted in a newspaper account, said, "Stopping building marinas is pretty big when you're the boating capital of the world."

Judith Vallee sees it as a necessary solution to a growing problem. "We're giving away our bottom lands in leases," she noted. "If a marina developer wants to build a dock out over the water, the state leases the submerged lands for a few cents a square foot, which is nothing. The bottom lands are owned by the state and its people— essentially they're like park lands. But special interest groups are making lots of money renting docks while negatively impacting our natural resources."

The DNR, which feels limited in its ability to control activities on submerged lands because of a lack of manpower and uncertainty as to their full enforcement authority, would like local governments to be responsible for adopting ordinances designed to regulate activities such as the use of jet skis and the construction of vessel anchorage areas and moorings over sovereign submerged lands. They would also like to strengthen their enforcement rights against unauthorized or illegal activities taking place on the state's submerged lands, specifically against unlicensed marine contractors who act as agents for the upland property owner. By forcing marine contractors to be licensed by the state, the DNR hopes to increase compliance with the laws governing the use of sovereign submerged lands.

Putting "more bite into the bark" is something manatee advocates have been wanting the state to do for years. When the Florida Manatee Sanctuary Act was passed in 1978, establishing the entire state as a "refuge and sanctuary for manatees," conservationists were hopeful that a turnaround in the fate of the manatee was at hand. But a lack of funding, political infighting, and powerful special interest groups have left the state's programs wallowing in bureaucracy while the manatee heads for an uncertain, if not fatal, future. In 1978, when the Sanctuary Act was passed, 86 manatees died. In 1991, 174 were found dead, 32 less than the previous year, which set a record.

Vallee believes that one of the key problem areas lies with marina developers and their noncompliance with laws designed to protect manatees. "The noncompliance rate is phenomenal," she said with visible anger. "There are all sorts of special conditions written into permits issued by the state to developers that are there to protect manatees: slow speed zones, the placement of educational displays, and a limit on the number of powerboat slips in the marina. The state can cancel a permit if the marina is not in compliance. But they've never done so! And the U.S. Fish and Wildlife Service recently reported a noncompliance rate of over sixty percent! All sorts of things have slipped through the cracks because no one was looking."

Finally, in the spring of 1990, the state legislature passed the Manatee Protection Bill, an amendment to the Sanctuary Act, that advocates felt was long overdue, giving the DNR more financial support, additional research personnel, and more control over the fate of the manatee through the ability to establish additional manatee protection zones as they see necessary. It also made the Inland Navigational Districts responsible for posting signs designed to alert boaters to special speed zones where manatees congregate. Yet bills to establish maximum statewide boat speed restrictions and mandatory boat operator's licenses failed at the same time.

At the center of the controversy over how much should be done to protect the manatee in Florida is the confusion over just how many of them really are left. For years the working number has been at least 1,200. Unfortunately, no matter how many die in a given year, the number has always remained the same, leading marine industry lobbyists to claim that the count was never correct in the first place.

"Years ago, the DNR said there were no more than five hundred manatees," said Ray. "Then they said there were no more than one thousand manatees. Two years ago they said there might be as many as twelve hundred. We believe," he concluded sarcastically, "that they were right all along and that manatees are growing in numbers."

"I think we have to get back to basics and find out what the manatee count is, period," added Lowe. "We have to establish a number. If you don't know where you are, how the hell do you know where you're going!"

Manatee advocates, concerned that the marine industry would use the number, whatever it is, to further their own goals, had been somewhat reluctant to do a full aerial survey.

"A full aerial survey of Florida is impossible to do," noted Dr. Dan Odell of Sea World. "You can fly the state but you'll never count them all due to weather, manatees submerged under vegetation, etc. The problem with doing a one- or two-time aerial survey is that you'll get a number and you'll have no idea what the statistical variation on that number is. So it's really meaningless. What concerns me, and everyone else dealing with manatees, is that biologically the number will be misinterpreted. It would be nice to have a proper survey, but I think the statistical variation would be so wide you wouldn't know what it means."

Vallee agrees. "No one really knows how many manatees in the wild it takes to make a viable population. Even if we come up with more animals than we expected, that does not make a strong population, nor does it indicate that the numbers have increased. It simply means that the aerial survey turned up more manatees." She added, "The marine industry has a hidden agenda. They're hoping that if we come up with more animals than the original estimate, they'll be able to say the manatee is not endangered, so you don't need to slow boats down, give manatees protection, or support them with tax dollars."

In early 1991, the DNR, after some effective lobbying by the boating industry, did take to the skies, performing two statewide aerial counts. The first effort, in January, turned up 1,268 manatees, but was hampered by foggy, windy weather. A month later, with improved visibility and cooperative weather, biologists counted 1,470 animals. In January 1992, another statewide survey was conducted with an estimated 1,856 manatees counted.

As Dr. Odell predicted, the numbers varied and will probably continue to do so with each successive count. At this time, neither side seems to be claiming victory for their respective causes as 1,856 animals by anyone's count is a paltry number of manatees, even considering the possibility that biologists may have missed a few hundred here or there. The reality is, there aren't a lot of manatees left in Florida. And with the population estimate still very meager and the reproductive rates so low, a massive loss of manatees, whether from natural or man-made causes, could strike a final blow to this gentle creature.

Besides the loss of habitat and increased boating activities, there are several other threats to manatees, including water pollution and litter. Herbicides, pesticides, and industrial chemicals ingested through their food or water can accumulate in manatee tissue and may have sublethal effects on the population. At this point, no one knows the long-range effects of this problem. (The use of copper-based herbicides to control vegetation along waterways is now restricted in areas where manatees congregate.)

Just as worrisome, and equally lethal, is the possibility of oil spills along Florida's fragile coast. In 1984 to 1985, the U.S. Department of the Interior sold seventy-three leases for oil drilling off South Florida to ten oil companies. But in the wake of the massive *Exxon Valdez* oil spill in Alaska and a dangerous tanker fire in the Gulf of Mexico, President Bush ordered a moratorium on exploration drilling on several sites around the country, including the area already leased off the Florida Keys. The president also instructed the Department of the Interior to "begin the cancellation of leases in the Florida Keys and to work with the state of Florida in an effort to jointly buy back the leases." Although the effort is sure to end up in lengthy legal battles—the Department has never had to cancel leases before—state officials are dead set against oil drilling off their coast, convinced it is not environmentally sound. The moratorium, however, is only for ten years, and should the oil companies win their case and a new energy crunch hit in another decade, oil drilling could return as an issue.

Existing oil tanker traffic is of immediate concern. Vessels carrying over 14 million tons of petroleum products pass by the south Florida coastline each year, oftentimes traveling close to reefs to avoid the treacherous Florida current. A massive oil spill could wipe out scores of manatees while also wreaking havoc on their fragile habitat. Fearing such an event, Florida officials have developed stricter regulations for responding to oil spills, with the legislature recently passing one of the country's most comprehensive oil spill laws. Still, in light of the *Exxon Valdez* accident, state environmentalists worry whether they can ever truly be fully prepared.

One of the more insidious killers of manatees could be one of the easiest problems to eliminate—litter. Each year, thousands of pounds of garbage including paper, wire, rope, discarded monofilament fishing line (which is almost invisible underwater), and fishing hooks end up in Florida's waterways. These items are accidently ingested by feeding manatees, with lethal effects. One U.S. Fish & Wildlife Service researcher found that out of 439 dead manatees examined in Brevard and Duval counties, on the state's north and central east coast, 61 of the animals had ingested a remarkable variety of debris including rubber bands, cellophane, fishing line, stockings, and plastic bags. The affected animals represented 14 percent of the study samples, a disturbingly high number of the population. Sharp items, such as metal wire or fish hooks, can directly cause death by puncturing internal organs. Monofilament fishing line or crabtrap lines entangled on manatee flippers or flukes can cause severe infections, amputation, or even death. These items are the normal residue of an active commercial- and sport-fishing industry. But if Florida's large sport fishing groups and commercial fisheries could be made to recognize that a greater environmental awareness is in their best interest, they could be a pivotal influence in educating the public and bringing about a widespread commitment to protecting the marine environment.

One of the more frightening threats to the statewide population of manatees is totally out of man's control—the occasional outbreaks of "red tide," a natural phenomenon caused by toxic, microscopic marine organisms called dinoflagellates. These microorganisms, which can sometimes be dense enough to color sea water red, are usually not lethal to marine mammals unless they ingest other forms of marine life with concentrated amounts of these toxic organisms. In the spring of 1982, just such a thing happened near Fort Myers, on the west coast, when thirty-seven manatees died in association with an outbreak of red tide. Biologists discovered that many of the dead manatees had accidently ingested significant numbers of toxic squirts, while feeding in the sea-grass beds. The incident brought to light the possibility of massive die-offs of manatees from future occurrences of red tide, offering dramatic proof of the fragility of the population.

A growing public awareness of the plight of the manatee has reduced some of the problems that earlier plagued the animals. Flood-control structures, such as flood gates and canal locks, once crushed or drowned numerous manatees, before modified operating procedures reduced such casualties. Hoop nets used by commercial fishermen along the St. John's River used to accidently drown calves before a simple excluder device improved the situation. And because of the animal's growing popularity, poaching and vandalism is becoming rarer. But one of the predictable results of this attention is an increase in harassment as more and more people flood to areas where the animals congregate. In state parks like Blue Spring, access to manatees is strictly controlled. But boaters, dock owners, or anyone near waterways where manatees are found are capable of harassing a manatee through actions as simple as throwing it a head of lettuce. Once wild animals know they can get easy food at a particular spot, they'll return time and time again until they begin to lose the inclination to move on to other natural feeding areas, initiating a pattern disruptive to their natural behavior that could end on a sad note. At Crystal River, Florida's most famous spot for swimming with manatees, the problem of harassment may be growing as more people choose to experience the fun of meeting these gentle creatures face to face.

After receiving various reports from friends and acquaintances about ever larger numbers of divers at Crystal River, I decided to make a return visit to see for myself, as I couldn't imagine that there could be more visitors there than I had seen on previous trips. Images of the crystalline spring waters and the large numbers of friendly manatees softened my recollections of my very first visit with Florida's mermaids so many years before. Somehow all the sad statistics and gloomy forecasts I gathered and heard over the years seemed to melt away as my expectations grew for another encounter with these fascinating creatures.

It was a beautifully clear, unseasonably warm February day that had been preceded by a long stretch of warm weather. I suspected that this weather pattern had effectively scattered the manatee population in Kings Bay. At the dive shop, though, it was painfully clear that everyone else's expectations remained remarkably high.

I was appalled by the sheer numbers of people gathered on the dock at that early hour, all pulling on rainbow-colored wetsuits, checking scuba tanks, or waiting in chatty groups for rental boats to be prepared. Charter buses vied for space with cars parked in every conceivable location. Diving groups from as far away as Mississippi elbowed for dock space with enthusiastic regional diving clubs. Motorized dive platforms were so densely packed that it seemed the slightest breeze would send them to the bottom sooner than expected.

The entrance to the dock was blocked by a large contingent of over outfitted divers, their pristine regulators and tanks glistening in the morning sun. Some fumbled with weight belts while others periodically checked their diving apparatus by letting piercing blasts of air escape from their regulators. Most looked and acted inexperienced, apparently satisfied that they were at least dressed to look the part. Most appeared to be under the age of forty.

I too was a player in this drama. I quickly chose a rental boat and headed for the southern part of Banana Island where I had often had good luck in viewing manatees. I was not to be disappointed. Despite silty water, I spent several hours observing the curious resting and feeding behavior of the many manatees who had moved into the bay to spend the winter. Later, as I sat in the boat, shivering within my soaked wetsuit, I watched a woman and a young girl sitting in a canoe throwing lettuce leaves to a couple of manatees who had been feeding on the bottom vegetation only moments before. The woman seemed totally unconcerned that I was watching her, despite the fact that feeding manatees is in violation of federal law and carries a stiff fine if the offender is convicted. And practically every piece of literature on manatees distributed by the state and federal governments for tourists and recreational divers warns against feeding manatees. The woman and child most certainly meant no harm, they no doubt thought they were doing the animals a favor, but biologists are adamant in stating that feeding manatees makes them too dependent on human handouts and too comfortable in the presence of boats and people, either one of which could harm them. This offense paled, however, next to the behavior I witnessed only two days later on a subsequent snorkeling trip to Crystal River.

I was curious to see if the silty water was a one-day phenomenon, so I returned to reconnoiter the bay. I rented a small boat and headed out against a stiff wind blowing out of the northeast. The temperature had dropped swiftly over the past couple of days and, despite the sunny skies, hovered in the forties, although the wind made it feel more like the twenties. I thought the sudden change in temperature might attract a large gathering of animals into the outlet of the main spring near the sanctuary, but I was wrong.

The chilly weather must have discouraged the usual crowds as there were hardly any divers on hand, only a few hardy souls moving about briskly on the anchored dive platforms, eager to dive into the warm waters of the bay.

I spent the first hour and a half snorkeling around the sanctuary, crisscrossing the area thoroughly, trying to find any sign of a manatee, a task made more difficult by the poor visibility. Schools of mullet dashed here and there, vanishing into the twilight haze through the wavering shafts of sunlight. Other than the schooling fish, the spring was empty. Finally, after my legs began to cramp and the chill grew more pervasive, I headed for the boat.

After a brief rest, I maneuvered the small craft around to the north side of Banana Island. Small choppy waves, whipped by the steady wind, slapped at the hull as I scanned the shallow depths less than 100 feet from the palm-laden shore of the island. I spotted a couple of snorkelers congregated in a small area that was distinctively outlined by a circular patch of light brown muddy water. As I watched them swim to and fro, I noticed two manatees surface in their midst. They had stumbled upon some resting manatees.

I sat and watched for a while as the lack of underwater visibility made their attempts to relocate the submerged manatees something like a comic opera. In the midst of the muddy cloud, a manatee surfaced, accompanied by frantic splashing as the snorkelers struggled to reach the animal before it submerged.

"He's over there!" they shouted, as they switched direction in a haphazard manner, kicking and thrashing to get near the animal. As soon as the manatee dove, always before the snorkelers could reach the spot, the intrepid tourists would spend the next couple of minutes spinning and twirling, facemasks in the water, hopelessly scanning the muddy spot where the manatee should have been but wasn't. Moments later, 30 yards away, a second animal surfaced, again setting off a frantic chase that ended in bitter disappointment for the snorkelers. And so it continued for quite some time, manatees seemingly surfacing everywhere but no one sighting anything because of the muddy waters.

Watching this humorous show, it was easy to believe that the manatees were a lot brighter than their human pursuers, eluding the annoying snorkelers with a deftness and alacrity that seemed to transcend mere animal instinct. Nevertheless, human persistence paid off. After a while, several snorkelers hovered next to the beleaguered manatees, stroking their gray, rubbery backs and chatting excitedly.

I waited for the group to leave before finally slipping into the water to get a closer look at the animals. There were four manatees in all, each rising rhythmically within a 50- to 60-foot diameter of clearly defined muddy water, that contrasted sharply with the greenish-blue water of the bay. I noticed one animal surface with rich, black mud pouring off its grizzly snout. Curious, I approached the mud-faced manatee slowly to see if I could figure out what it was doing to stir up so much sediment. Visibility was near zero. At one point I could have bumped into a submarine and not known the difference.

As I stared into the water, trying to make some sense out of the silty chaos in front of my face, an eerie feeling of fear washed over me. There I was, all by myself, a good distance offshore, in brown water with several half ton animals hiding somewhere beneath the surface, perhaps inches from my fins, and my boat drifting 30 yards away. All those questions I've been asked about alligators and their unpredictable habits suddenly seemed less idiotic and very disconcerting.

I was startled from my pipe dreams by the appearance of a face out of the gloom, mere inches from my facemask. Its push-button eyes, prickly pear snout, and friendly grin relieved any concerns about reptilian reprisals. Instead, its curiosity seemed to invite contact as it held its position in front of me, staring my way in a trance-like stupor. As if accepting its imagined invitation, I reached out and stroked its calloused back. Clouds of silt billowed up off its skin at my touch. Its tiny eyes never wavered as it stared into the reflective glass of my facemask. Finally, its curiosity satiated, it broke the surface for a quick breath and then descended like a stone, plunking onto the muddy bottom with a cloud-raising thud. Not wishing to disturb the animal any further, I swam off.

By this time a diving platform loaded with several divers moved into the area and headed in my direction, leaving a distinct trail of evenly spaced bubbles at the surface. When the leader discovered a resting manatee in a clearer area of water, he quickly surfaced to call the others, still on the platform, over. Like moths to a flame, six or seven divers surrounded the single animal, stroking its back, patting its head, and grabbing at its tail. It was clear that the animal was disturbed by all the fuss. When it moved swiftly to another spot 10 or 15 yards away, the group zealously followed it, grabbing at its flippers and continually stroking its sides and back. The dismay I felt at having allowed the group to find the animal soon turned to anger.

During the next seven to eight minutes, the divers had chased the animal to four or five different locations, at times holding onto its tail as it rushed to get away. As I treaded water nearby, watching the drama unfold, all the divers surfaced at once only a few feet away. The leader took the regulator out of his mouth and asked if they had had enough of this particular animal, as if it were some meal to be devoured. Several of them asked for more. "I'll go down and force him to the surface," he proclaimed, hell-bent on providing his people with a good time, regardless of the world effect on the animal. He proceeded to do just that, pulling at the animal's tail and flippers, literally trying to tug the animal up off the bottom. Obligingly, the hapless creature rose, much to the group's delight. Several minutes passed and the divers suddenly swam off and left, apparently satisfied that they had conquered the wild kingdom well enough for one day.

I have witnessed such episodes on practically all my visits to Crystal River, although none to the extreme of this one. But if I'm seeing such encounters fairly commonly, it's probably safe to assume that they happen with an alarming amount of frequency. Are the divers and snorkelers in Crystal River having an adverse effect on the population of manatees there?

During the winters of 1987, 1988, and 1989, Cheryl Buckingham of the Florida Cooperative Fish and Wildlife Research Unit, U.S. Fish & Wildlife Service, conducted a study to determine what effect, if any, human activity was having on the three hundred or so manatees that use Crystal River and Kings Bay as a winter refuge. Her study concluded that the number of boats and people in the South Bay altered the way manatees use that habitat, causing a significant disruption of normal behavioral patterns. Her recommendations included the creation of additional sanctuaries there, limiting the number of boats, and increased law enforcement. But will it be enough?

To listen to the story of the manatee in Florida is to face the issues that will determine the future of thousands of endangered species worldwide. It's a matter of development versus protection, supply versus the demand for more space for more people in a world that's shrinking beneath the pressures of population daily. The story is a gloomy one but not altogether hopeless.

I find it incomprehensible that anyone could hate or even dislike manatees. I'm not sure anyone does. But for some people in Florida they and the people who fight to protect them represent a stumbling block to the traditional concept of "progress," where the freedom to develop, expand, and recreate as they see fit is based in the very foundations of American ideology. Yet, at some point, someone has to sit down and define just how much freedom is too much freedom, a complex concept that seems far beyond the scope of a leadership that bases its decisions more on narrow-minded political considerations than on doing what's right for the people as a whole.

In other parts of the world where fragment populations of manatees remain, the issues are similar—population pressures, increased development, growing pollution—but the financial capability to make a difference is not. In many parts of West Africa, South America, Central America, and the Caribbean, manatees have been reduced to small localized populations, hunted by the natives who convert the meat and bones into much needed currency. For many of them, it's a matter of survival, not conservation.

Dugongs face an even wider spectrum of problems simply because their range is so vast and varied. There's no way to determine the total population of dugongs worldwide. Even if some sort of a count could ever be attempted, what, would it tell us? The number of dugongs that exist now? Hardly likely. How many dugongs there once were? No. Like the recent Florida count, it could only give a vague idea of how many might be swimming out there. We wouldn't know whether the population was thriving or dying out. Nor could we tell how many dugongs constitute a healthy population. Scientists generally believe that Australia, where dugong populations are counted in the thousands, may be the last hope for the survival of the species. Infrequent sightings and habitat destruction throughout the rest of the Indo-Pacific region make it very likely that dugongs will soon disappear from those areas.

The recent war in the Persian Gulf brought to light a new, more frightening form of warfare that could spell extinction for the dugong and many other endangered animals living in the shadow of politically unstable countries. When Saddam Hussein unleashed an estimated 294 million gallons of crude oil into the Persian Gulf, he not only endangered the world's second-largest known population of dugongs, estimated recently at seven thousand animals, he initiated a new type of warfare that some environmentalists refer to as "eco-war." The oil release was almost thirty times the size of the *Exxon Valdez* oil spill. And for an 88,000–square-mile sea that averages only 114 feet in depth, the consequences could be catastrophic. Until the fall of 1991 the oil fields he set ablaze continued to burn, the burning fuel falling as black, greasy rain over the vast expanse of desert and the Gulf. The long-term effects of such madness will not be known for some time. But already the floating oil slick has wreaked havoc on one of the world's most beautiful and delicate ecosystems, prompting *Time* magazine to call it a "dead sea in the making."

Such ecological disasters support a recent National Science Foundation study that estimated that more than one quarter of the earth's species of animals, plants, microbes, and fungi will become extinct if measures aren't taken immediately to preserve them. The foundation estimated that about 1.4 million species have been identified and named throughout the world, with the possibility that the total number of species may range from 5 million to 80 million. Some biologists believe that the current rate of habitat destruction is causing one to three extinctions daily, with the rate increasing to one extinction *per hour* by the end of this century.

Will the manatee become a part of these sad statistics? Many biologists and conservationists believe the possibility exists. They have long used the argument that the plight of the manatee is nothing more than a symptom of the overall illness; as the manatee goes, so goes the state's natural resources. Marine industry lobbyists scoff at the idea, sticking to the belief that there are more manatees out there than we are led to believe. That may be so, but the bottom line is that manatees in Florida are dying in record numbers, and there is much to be done to stem the tide. There has got to be a middle ground where federal and state officials, environmentalists, and marine industry interests can meet to solve the problems. If we can't save manatees in this country, what hope is there for manatees and dugongs in the rest of the world where conservation and political stability are only vague concepts or idealistic dreams?

Florida and its manatees stand as a symbol, a microcosm of a larger problem facing the earth and its limited resources. Can modern man and his rapid-fire technology coexist with a creature that harkens back to a world where nature, and nature alone, controlled fate? Swimming at its sleepy pace in the land of sunshine, the manatee is an anachronism, a throwback to an era long lost in the misty passages of a time before man walked the earth. Its survival to date was dependent on the process of natural selection. But as we have shaped, molded, and conformed our world to serve the needs of a growing population, we've removed the mantle of responsibility from the delicate chain of natural forces. Now, the fate of the mythical mermaids is in our hands.

SELECTED READING

Anderson, Paul K. "Dugongs of Shark Bay, Australia—Seasonal Migration, Water Temperature, and Forage." *National Geographic Research* (Autumn 1986): 473–489.

The Australian Encyclopaedia. City, South Australia: The Australian Geographic Society, 1988.

Bertram, Colin. *In Search of Mermaids: The Manatees of Guiana.* New York: Thomas Y. Crowell Company, 1963.

Bonner, William Hallam. *Captain William Dampier, Buccaneer-Author.* Stanford, CA: Stanford University Press, 1934

Bradley, Richard. *The Pre-Columbian Exploitation of the Manatee in Mesoamerica.* Cambridge, MA: A Report at the Harvard University Library, 1983.

Brazil, Jeff. "The First Year of the Last Decade: Manatee." *Orlando Sentinel: Special Report* (December 16, 1990):1–12.

Cousteau, Jean-Michel. "Eco-War in the Gulf." *Calypso Log* (April 1991): 3.

Cropp, Ben. Timeless Hunters." *Oceans* (November 1982): 17–20.

Dampier, William. *A New Voyage Round the World*. London: James Knapton, At the Crown in St. Paul's Church-yard, 1697.

Domning, Daryl P. "Marching Teeth of the Manatee." *Natural History* (May 1983): 8–11.

Domning, Daryl P. "Sea Cow Family Reunion." *Natural History* (April 1987): 64–71.

Domning, Daryl P. *Sirenian Evolution in the North Pacific Ocean*. Berkeley: University of California Press, 1978.

Douglas, Sue. "To Save a Vanishing Floridian." *Oceans* (November–December 1982): 8–15.

Duplaix, Nicole. "South Florida Water: Paying the Price." *National Geographic* (July 1990): 89–113.

Ehrlich, Paul. "Stemming the Human Tide." *Calypso Log* (February 1991): 16–18.

Ellis, Sara L. "An Explanation for the Dolphin Die-Off." *Oceanus* (Spring 1989): 79.

Fleming, Carrol B. "Maidens of the Sea Can Be Alluring, But Sailor, Beware." *Smithsonian* (June 1983): 86–95.

Ford, Corey. *Where the Sea Breaks its Back*. Boston: Little, Brown and Company, 1966.

Fox, Rodney. "The Coast of Northwest Australia: The Sea Beyond the Outback." *National Geographic* (January 1991): 42–73.

Greenwell, Richard, ed. "New Expedition Identifies Ri as Dugong." *The ISC Newsletter* (Spring 1985): 1–3.

Greenwell, Richard, ed. "New Guinea Expedition Observes Ri." *The ISC Newsletter* (Summer 1983): 1–2.

Grigione, Melissa M., and James A. Powell. *Manatees in Korup National Park*. A report submitted to the World Wildlife Fund, November 30, 1989.

Grizmek, Dr. H. C. Bernhard. *Grizmek's Animal Life Encyclopedia*. New York: Van Nostrand Reinhold Company, 1972.

Hartman, Daniel S. "Ecology and Behavior of the Manatee (*Trichechus manatus*) in Florida." *Special Publication No. 5*, the American Society of Mammalogists, 1979.

Hartman, Daniel S. "Florida's Manatees: Mermaids in Peril." *National Geographic* (September 1969): 342–353.

Hendrickson, Robert. *The Ocean Almanac*. New York: Doubleday & Company, 1984.

Heuvelmans, Bernard. *In the Wake of the Sea-Serpents*. New York: Hill and Wang, 1968.

Husar, Sandra L. "The Dugong: Endangered Siren of the South Seas." *National Parks & Conservation* (February 1975): 15–18.

Kipling, Rudyard. *The Jungle Books*. New York: NAL Penguin, 1981.

Marsh, Helene, ed. *The Dugong: Proceedings of a Seminar/Workshop held at James Cook University 8–13 May 1979*. North Queensland, New Zealand: James Cook University of North Queensland, Department of Zoology, 1981.

Morison, Samuel Eliot. *Admiral of the Ocean Sea: A Life of Christopher Columbus*. Boston: Little, Brown and Company, 1942.

Nietschmann, Bernard, and Judith Nietschmann. "Good Dugong, Bad Dugong; Bad Turtle, Good Turtle." *Natural History* (May 1981): 54–63.

Odom, R. R., K. A. Riddleberger, and J. C. Ozier, eds. "The Past, Present, and Future of Manatees in the Southeastern United States: Realities, Misunderstandings, and Enigmas." In *Proceedings of the Third Southeastern Nongame and Endangered Wildlife Symposium*, 1988, pp. 184–204.

Parker, Patricia A. "No More Drilling: Read My Lips." *Sea Frontiers* (September–October 1990): 13–19.

Pomet, Monsieur. *A Compleat History of Drugs*. London: J. and J. Bonwicke, R. Wilkin, S. Birt, T. Ward and E. Wicksteed, 1737.

Reynolds, John E., III, and Daniel K. Odell. *Manatees and Dugongs*. New York: Facts on File, 1991.

Ridgway, Sam H., and Richard Harrison. *Handbook of Marine Mammals, Volume 3: The Sirenians and Baleen Whales*. London: Academic Press, 1985.

Romance of the Sea. Washington, DC: The National Geographic Society, 1981.

Scheffer, Victor B. "The Last Days of the Sea Cow." *Smithsonian* (January 1973): 64–67.

Shaw, John. *The Collins Australian Encyclopedia*. Sydney: John Shaw and Associates, 1984.

Shoumatoff, Alex. *The Rivers Amazon*. San Francisco: Sierra Club Books, 1978.

Steller, Georg Wilhelm. *Journal of a Voyage with Bering 1741–1742*. Stanford, CA: Stanford University Press, 1988.

Strahan, Ronald. *The Complete Book of Australian Mammals*. Sydney: Angus & Robertson Publishers, 1983.

Stone, Roger D. *Dreams of Amazonia*. New York: Viking, 1985.

Stuart, George E., and Gene S. Stuart. *The Mysterious Maya*. Washington, DC: National Geographic Society, 1977.

U.S. Fish and Wildlife Service. Florida Manatee (Trichechus manatus latirostris) Recovery Plan. Atlanta, GA: Prepared by the Florida Manatee Recovery Team of the U.S. Fish and Wildlife Service, 1989.

Van Meter, Victoria Brook. *The West Indian Manatee in Florida*. Miami: Florida Power and Light Company, 1989.

Verne, Jules. *The Mysterious Island*. Garden City, NY: Dolphin Books, Doubleday & Co., 1961.

Vietmeyer, Noel. "The Endangered but Useful Manatee." *Smithsonian* (December 1974): 60–65.

Williams, Thomas R. "Identification of the Ri Through Further Fieldwork in New Ireland, Papua, New Guinea." *Crytozoology: Interdisciplinary Journal of The International Society of Cryptozoology*. (Volume 4, 1985): 61–68.

INDEX

SINCE 1974, MORE THAN 1800 MANATEES HAVE DIED IN FLORIDA

Time is running out
Help support manatee conservation efforts by sending your
tax-deductible contribution to:

SAVE THE MANATEE® CLUB
500 N. Maitland Ave., Maitland, FL 32751
Or call for further information
1-800-432-JOIN

Funds raised go toward public awareness, education, research, and
lobbying efforts.